Decoding Indian Economy

Goenkans

pencil

ISBN 978-93-5610-672-7

Published in India 2022 by Pencil

Contributors:
Editor: Dr Priyanka Raheja
Editor: Ms. Manjari Arora
Editor: Ms. Vanshika Bansal
Co-Author: Mr. Jai Aneja
Co-Author: Ms.Nisha Aneja
Co-Author: Ms.Priyanshi Gupta
Co-Author: Ms.Vanshika Bansal
Co-Author: Mr.Ayan Jain
Co-Author: Mr.Samarth Sarthak Shandilya
Co-Author: Ms. Saniya Gupta
Co-Author: Ms. Ishanvie Bansal
Co-Author: Ms. Mehak Malhotra
Co-Author: , Ms. Tanish Poddar
Co-Author: Mr. Raghav M Garg
Co-Author: Ms. Uditi Gupta
Co-Author: Ms. Mehak Gupta
Co-Author: Ms.Anya Jain
Co-Author: Ms.Pihu Goel
Illustrator: Ms.Ramya Arora
Translator: Professor Sanjay Rout

A brand of
One Point Six Technologies Pvt. Ltd.
123, Building J2, Shram Seva Premises,
Wadala Truck Terminal, Wadala (E)
Mumbai 400037, Maharashtra, INDIA
E connect@thepencilapp.com
W www.thepencilapp.com

Author biography

The book is written by Goenkans Edited by Dr. Priyanka Raheja, Co-edited by Ms. Manjari Arora , Student Editor is Ms. Vanshika Bansal & Illustrator is Ms.Ramya Arora. The books all authors(Mr.Jai Aneja,Ms.Priyanshi Gupta,Ms.Vanshika Bansal,Mr.Ayan Jain,Samarth Sarthak Shandilya,Ms. Saniya Gupta,Ms.Ishanvie Bansal,Ms.Mehak Malhotra,Ms.Tanisha Poddar,Mr.Raghav M Garg,Ms.Uditi Gupta,Ms.Mehak Gupta, Ms.Anya Jain , Ms.Pihu Goel) are from G.D.Goenka Public School Rohini, Sector 22, Delhi (India).

CONTENTS

Epigraph

The book Decoding Indian Economy covers various aspects of the Indian Economy including its problems along with suggested solutions. This book is a compilation of research done by students who were sensitized by news articles related to the contemporary Indian Economy. We present this book as a guide to help the researchers and graduate students in the commerce writing research papers. The ideas presented, intended to facilitate further research in the relevant field. The book is written by GOENKANS Edited by Dr. Priyanka Raheja, Co-edited by Ms. Manjari Arora , Student Editor is Ms. Vanshika Bansal & Illustrator done by Ms.Ramya Arora . The book published by ISL Publications

Foreword

Ms. Anuradha Pant has an experience of over 28 years in the education circuit. She has been instrumental in the formulation and implementation of institutional policies, Strategic Operations Management and in providing academic leadership in curriculum designing, promoting child centric pedagogies and learner evolution. Hailing from the Defence elite, Ms. Pant has had the opportunity of exploring diversities and thus upholds her strong faith in ethical values. She has therefore been propagating the idea of Emotional Intelligence and Scientific Attitude and bringing Life Skills to the classroom.

Ms. Pant served as an active member of Sahodaya, the team commissioned to formulate and implement Continuous and Comprehensive Evaluation System in schools. She has been awarded with the prestigious 'Young Achievers Award' by the Chief Minister of Chhattisgarh for her remarkable contribution in the field of education. Besides, she has also been recognized as the 'Best Teacher' by C.M.S, Lucknow. She has been associated as a Chemistry specialist in schools of repute such as City Montessori School, Lucknow; KV; Amity International, Noida; D.R.S. Hyderabad and Mayor School under the aegis of Mayo College, Ajmer. The schools under her able guidance recorded an unprecedented rise in academic performance index. As a Debater herself at University

Level and also a National level Athlete, not only has she enhanced the academic standards of the school, but has also placed an equal emphasis on co-curricular activities and sports. She has presented papers and published several articles on C.C.E. and Educational reforms and pedagogy. As a YLE Trainer of The Cambridge English Program, she has nurtured in pupils, the love for language. And currently as the Principal of GDGPS, Sector 22, Rohini, she continues to stride ahead and set higher benchmarks of achievement.

Preface

Dr. Priyanka Raheja

On 14 August 1947, Nehru had declared: "Long years ago we made a tryst with destiny, and now the time comes when we shall redeem our pledge. The achievement we celebrate today is but a step, an opening of opportunity, to the great triumph and achievements that await us." He reminded the country that the tasks ahead included "the ending of poverty and ignorance and disease and inequality of opportunity". These were the basic foundations on which India embarked upon its path of development since gaining independence in 1947.

Now the question that arises is, how much has India really achieved in fulfilling the aspirations on which it was founded, as we are approaching the 75th year of independence? This book is by students and teachers of G.D.Goenka is a small step to answer this .In the wake of the pandemic, this book reflects what Indians experience and transact with today.Topics have been chosen keeping in mind that India is still struggling to come out of the economic morass.

Moody's Investors Service in its latest report has projected that the economic growth in India will rebound strongly. It has pegged GDP growth for the nation at 9.3% and 7.9% in FY22 and FY23, respectively. However, we must not forget that India will take time to terms with the disruptions caused by the virus. It is now clear that the pandemic has brought the world to the second great economic and financial crisis of the 21st century and is likely to have long-term structural repercussions. What's more, it has laid bare the fragilities of the global economic and geopolitical order.In this book we have tried to take cover topics like employment, sustainable development, medical tourism, BOP has been covered in the book which is crucial in shaping a new India with a better future for all.

On the global stage, India's diplomatic efforts are driven by the philosophy of vasudhaivakutumbakam - the world is one family. This is the kind of narrative our students have adopted in this book. Indeed, India's call for renewed and reformed multilateralism is resonating with global leaders and policy-makers and our Goenkans are torch bearers for the same.

Dr. PRIYANKA RAHEJA (Editor)
Educator, India, Dedicated and goal-driven professional educator with a strong commitment to the social and academic growth and development of every child. Dr. Priyanka is highly motivated, enthusiastic and dedicated educator who wants all children to be successful learners. As a self-directed, action-oriented professional with over 15 years of experience in education and community

service, she has proven abilities in problem solving, people management and motivation.

Ms. ManjariArora (Co-Editor)
Educator at G.D. Goenka Public School, Sec-22, Rohini, she has an experience of over 12 years . As a successful researcher, she has always been interested ingathering evidences for theories and developing knowledge of study. Being a people's person , sympathetic and a quick thinker, she has the ability to analyse the situation and work in a collaborative environment.

Ms. Vanshika Bansal (Student-Editor)
Author, Student and Researcher at 16,studying in GD Goenka Public School Rohini sector-22, immensely passionate about writing , she takes interest in learning about new cultures and sharing her experiences with others.

Ms. Nisha Aneja
An adept Educator and keen observer with around two decades of experience of enthusiastically engaging with senior school learners, Ms. Nisha Aneja, currently leading the Senior School division of G.D. Goenka Public School, Rohini Sector 22 is an alumnus of the prestigious Daulat Ram College of University of Delhi.

Acknowledgements

We would like to express our special thanks to our principal Ms. Anuradha Pant and senior in-charge, Ms. Nisha Aneja, to encourage us and provide us the opportunity to facilitate the research and record the same in writing. We express heartfelt gratitude to them.

We acknowledge our guide, Dr. Priyanka Raheja, whose valuable guidance and kind supervision throughout the course shaped the present work.

Analysis of Medical Tourism in India

First Author Bio:
Mr. Jai Aneja is an enthusiastic learner, is fond of research and field work. His zeal to learn new concepts and apply them in reality makes him an outstanding learner.

Second Author Bio:
Ms.Nishs Aneja is an adept Educator and keen observer with around two decades of experience of enthusiastically engaging with senior school learners, Ms. Nisha Aneja, currently leading the Senior School division of G.D. Goenka Public School, Rohini Sector 22 is an alumnus of the prestigious Daulat Ram College of University of Delhi.

Analysis of Medical Tourism in India

Abstract:

With medical tourism being an important impactor of health care provision and enhancement as well as a contributor the world economy, India has emerged as an attractive place for this growing sector. Tourists in India receive affordable treatment, quality healthcare and world class facilities. This paper analysis medical tourism in India and the impact it has laid on the economy.

Introduction:

What is medical tourism?
Medical tourism is the practice of travelling abroad for medical treatment. In general, it is the travel of people to another country for the purpose of obtaining medical treatment in that country.
Medical tourism can be broadly defined as provision of 'cost effective' private medical care in collaboration with the tourism industry for patients needing surgical and other forms of specialized treatment. This process is being facilitated by the corporate sector involved in medical care as well as the tourism industry - both private and public.

Why India?
India offers World Class Facilities, comparable with any of the western countries. India has state of the art Hospitals and the best qualified doctors. With the best infrastructure, the best possible Medical Facilities, accompanied with the most competitive prices, you can get the treatment done in India at the lowest charges. India is in the process of becoming the "Global Health Destination".
Low Cost
Offshore medical procedures are conducted for as much as 1/10th the cost of a comparable treatment in developed countries due to the economic disparity.
A bone marrow transplant which would cost you around $250,000 in the US and mere $25,000 in India. A patient can successfully get a gastric bypass surgery in India by paying just $9,500 as against a $65,000 price tag for the same in the US. It is also a good idea to avail a medial tourism package which would include airfare,

accommodation charges and a visit to some of the holiday destinations in the country.

Less waiting time

Private health care in India is comparable to much that is available at the best hospitals in the world and at a far lower cost. Even considering the cost of air travel and luxury hotel accommodation (if required), the cost savings comes out to be 40-80 % of what is in the USA.

World Class Facilities

High quality healthcare

Experienced and talented pool of Medical Professionals

Strong private hospital infrastructure

English is widely spoken

Familiarity of western patients with Indian doctors

Rich Cultural Heritage

Snow clad mountain peaks of mighty Himalayas, verdant hill stations, breath taking beaches, lovely lakes, gushing waterfalls, enchanting rivers, scenic backwaters, magnificent monuments, cultural heritage, fantastic forts, elegant places terrific temples, intricate churches, colonial homes, wildlife parks & sanctuary, bird sanctuaries, dense forests, beautiful landscapes and of course generous peoples comprise the amazing and magical land called India. Hospitals in India Impact Medical Tourism on the Indian Economy.

India has almost everything which is necessary for a prime tourism destination in the world. The Prime elements of Indian Tourism are Culture tourism, adventure tourism, wildlife tourism, heritage tourism, monument tourism, beach tourism, hill station tourism, backwater tourism, nature tourism, eco-tourism, village tourism, medical tourism, monsoon tourism, etc are appeal tourists from all over the world for India tours and travel. During your travel you will have a brilliant opportunity to observe rich culture and civilization of the country.

Hospitals in India

AIIMS

APOLLO

B.M BIRLA HEART RESEARCH CENTRE

ESCORTS HOSPITAL AND RESEARCH CENTRE

TATA MEMORIAL HOSPITAL

APOLLLO CANCER HOSPITAL

INDRAPRASTHA MEDICAL CORPORATION

Impact of Medical Tourism on the Indian economy

According to a study by global accounting and consulting firm Ernst and Young and the Federation of Indian Chambers of Commerce and Industry (FICCI), private hospitals in India earned Rs.62,000 crores in fiscal 2006 and revenues from the sector are expected to rise up to Rs.1,30,000 crores (at current prices and exchange rates) in 2012, which represents an annual revenue growth rate of about 19 percent a year.

After Information Technology and Information Technology enables Services, which are currently good contributors to our nation's G.D.P, the next big thing happening (already begun) could be "Medical Tourism", which has enormous potential, if rightly tapped, to make great contributions to the nation's G.D.P.

Conclusion:

India is emerging as an attractive and affordable place for healthcare. But there are some challenges that the country has to overcome to become a tourist destination with competent health care industry. The government should step in the role of a regulator and a facilitator of private investment in healthcare. An apex body for the industry needs to be formed to promote the India brand abroad and aid inter-sectoral coordination. Joint ventures with overseas partners and establishment of MEDICITIES will help in India building a significant advantage and leadership position in the industry.

Role of Informal Credit Sector in India

Ms. Priyanshi Gupta
Author Bio: Ms.Priyanshi Gupta is a Author, student researcher and entrepreneur at 16 studying in GD Goenka public school immensely passionate about writing. She is positive, helpful, friendly and determined towards the work allotted to her. She takes interest in learning and sharing ideas.

Abstract:

Two facets of urban informal credit market have been recognised by various author one, that informal credit largely serves differing needs of low-income households, and two that under the circumstances in which current credit market functions, informal suppliers are at a disadvantage and have several shortcomings. Various approaches have been attempted from promulgation of targeted credit programmes for the low-income households, to active legislation that has attempted to curb the functioning of ICM suppliers. The paper lists 14 features of the ICM that has enabled it to effectively reach the urban poor, and draws implications for microcredit programmes that are targeted at such groups.

Key words:

Informal credit, microcredit, slum and squatter settlements, development countries, India, policy and programme development.

Introduction:

Many developing countries, despite double digit growth rates, have lagged far behind in terms of quality of living in urban areas. Problems of unemployment, inadequate housing, poor environmental quality, rampant crime, poverty, transportation etc. have plagued urban residents and decision makers alike. While the attempts of governmental agencies have been commendable, sheer scale of the problem has diluted such efforts, resulting in the benefits being spread thinly among a large population, or not benefiting most of them.
Low-income households in developing countries are seen as particularly vulnerable. Their personal problems of low education and skill levels, low incomes, lack of marketable assets, and uncertain job markets have been compounded by external factors that have failed to provide adequate infrastructure and social services that would have enabled them to participate in mainstream economic activities. As a result, this has affected every facet of their life: employment (predominantly in the informal sector), education (non-existent or up to primary levels only), health (low quality or traditional), housing (impermanent materials and illegal settlements) etc.

Often the problems of low-income households can be

traced back to a single factor which, on a cumulative basis, has affected other factors, resulting in their present condition. For low income households, one such cumulating factor is credit, or the lack of access to adequate bank credit. This lack of access has resulted in households turning to informal credit markets (ICMs) to satisfy their need, where elaborate networks of credit delivery have been set up by different kinds of informal suppliers. Examples include money lenders, pawn brokers, ROSCAs, credit societies/unions etc.

Objectives:
1. To identify the characteristics of IMC.
2. To study which type of credit loan is better and which class of people avail them.
3. To analyse the reasons why poor uses the Informal credit market.

Literature Review :
Akshita Verma, an employee in an Expression Salon, has to take a loan of Rs.5 lakhs from the bank to purchase a house. The annual interest rate on the loan is 12% and is to be repair in 10 years in monthly instalments. She had to submit to the bank, documents showing her employment records and salary before the bank agreed to give her the loan. Bank retained as collateral the paper of the new house, which will be returned to Akshita once the entire loan is repaid. In the fear of bad dept and losing her only one property she decided to take loan

from her friend which provided her the loan of Rs. 5 lakhs without asking for collateral and no such time limit.
Rama Yadav, a small farmer in Kalap Uttarakhand, approach to the bank for the loan to buy the farm input. Midway through the season the crop was hit by pest and the crops fail. He was unable to repay the loan but since he hasn't repaid the previous loan, the bank wasn't willing to lend him further.

What is informal credit?

The Informal sources include all small and scattered units that are generally beyond the government's control and charge much higher interest rate for informal sources. The profit making is the primary motive for this source. Informal credit operations involving lending, generally at short term, among friends, relatives, landlords, neighbours, shopkeepers, farmers, village moneylenders and other local income groups.

The following aspects characterise the ICM:

Scale of operations is small, because lending is primarily based on personal knowledge of the borrower. Loans are small, repaid quickly, and are largely unsecured.
Due to the small scale of operations, intra agency problems typical of large organisations like banks are not seen in the ICM.
Suppliers function outside the purview of regulations imposed in the formal sector in respect of capital, reserve and liquidity requirements, ceilings on lending and deposit rates, mandatory credit targets, audit and reporting

requirements and so on.

Reasons why the poor use the informal credit market

1. It does not require a license
2. It facilitates very small savings behaviour
3. It is not non-profit motivated
4. It has strong organisational structure
5. It does not need collateral
6. It is not regulated by the central bank

Data Analysis

Graph 1:

People obtain loans from various sources. The various types of loan can be conveniently grouped as formal sector loan and informal sector loan. In the following pie chart (Graph 1) ,We can clearly see that more than half of the people prefer to take loan from formal credit sector than informal credit sector. This is because RBI supervises the functioning of formal sources of loan. Banks have to submit information to RBI on how much they are lending to whom, at what interest rate etc. There is no organisation which supervises the credit activities
of lenders in the Informal sector. They can lend at whatever interest rate they choose.

According to you, which class majorly depend on informal sector?

Graph 2:

(Graph 2)Collateral is an asset that the borrower owns and uses this as a guarantee to a lender until the loan is repaid. Interest rate, collateral and documentation requirement and the mode of repayment together comprise what is called the terms of credit. Rich people owns property such as building, vehicle etc. so can get the credit from formal sources. Absence of banks and cooperative societies in the rural area, collateral, documents and lack of awareness the poor class of the society have to take loan from informal sector credit. That's why poor people are majorly dependent on informal sector.

Do you think informal credit sector have any impact on national income of a country?

Graph 3 :

In the above pie chart (graph 3) represents the most of people agree with the fact that informal credit sector have an impact on nation income of the country. Informal economy not only contribute to economic growth but the firm also help to significantly reduce inflation by generating employment and hence maintain political stability in the economy.

Graph 4:

The shoe manufacturer, Shyam, has received an order from a large trader in town for 3,000 pairs of shoes to be delivered in a month time. To complete production on time, Shyam has to hire a few more workers for stitching and pasting work. He has to purchase the raw materials. To meet these expenses, Shyam obtains loans from two sources. First, he asks the leather supplier to supply leather now and promises to pay him later. Second, he obtains loan in cash from the large trader as advance payment for 1000 pairs of shoes with a promise to deliver the whole order by the end of the month.

At the end of the month, Shyam is able to deliver the order, make a good profit, and repay the money that he had borrowed.

So in the above case it tells how informal credit loan helps Shyam (refer to graph 4) without demanding collateral to complete his order on time and he was able to make a good profit.

Conclusion:

The market structure of informal credit supply and demand provides valuable insight for the designing of effective microcredit programmes targeted at low income households. Three key lessons emerge from the 14 reasons mentioned above. Firstly, due to localised services, specific borrowers, personalised services and close informational links, credit supplied by the ICM is timely. Secondly, strong organisational structures, non-profit motives, opportunities for very small savings and other features encourage borrowers to save. Many credit groups provide loans only if a specified amount is saved by the member/borrower. Thirdly, the terms and conditions of loans made by informal suppliers are very flexible. These are worked out on a mutually agreed formula, and even within a credit cycle, it can be modified to suit the changing socio-economic status of the borrower. Further research is indeed necessary in understanding adaptability of ICM features into mainstream microcredit programmes, as well as other factors that affect such programmes. Of particular significance for study is the role of NGOs, both local and international, as intermediaries and animators in developing microcredit programmes for low-income households. NGOs have greater flexibility and adaptability in developing their programmes. The process of NGO intervention into low-income communities on one hand, and the adoption and incorporation of positive ICM features into microcredit programmes needs further study

References:

ADB (1990), "Informal Finance in Asia". Asian Development Outlook 1990, Manila: Asian Development Bank, pp. 187 215.

ADB (1991) The Urban Poor and Basic Infrastructure Services in Asia and the Pacific. Proceedings of a Regional Seminar. January 22-28 1991, Manila, Philippines.

Devas, Nick (1983) "Financing Urban Land Development for Low-Income Housing: An Analysis with Particular reference to Jakarta, Indonesia". Third World Planning Review. Vol. 5, No. 3, August 1983.

Fuchs et al. (1994), Mega-city growth and the future. Tokyo: United Nations University Press.

Germicides, Dimitri, Denis Kessler and Rachel Meghir (1991), Financial Systems and Development: What Role for the Formal and Informal Financial Sectors? Development Centre Studies. Paris: OECD

Ghate, Prabhu, Informal Finance: Some Findings from Asia. Economic and development Resource Centre. Manila: Asian Development Bank, 1990.

Gilbert, Alan and Ann Varley (1990), "Renting a Home in a Third World City: Choice or Constraint". International Journal of Urban and Regional Research. Vol. 14, No. 1, March 1990.

de Groot, Han and Otto Hospes (1988), Policy Guidelines for NGOs Involved in Savings and Credit Schemes. The Hague: NederlandseOrganisatievoor Internationale Ontwikkelingssamcnwerking (NOVIB), June, 38 pp.

Gupta, Anil (1987), "Banks NGO Poor Interface in Backward Regions: Alternatives for Action". Draft document.

Hopkins, Elwood, The Life Cycle of Urban Innovations. UMP Working Paper 2. Washington D.C.: UNCHS/WB/UNDP Urban Management Programme, 1994.

Analysis of India's BOP Position

Ms.Vanshika Bansal
Author Bio: Author Ms.Vanshika Bansal, Student Researcher at 16,studying in GD GoenkaPublic School Rohini sector-22, immensely passionate about writing. She takes interest in learning about new cultures and sharing her experiences with others

Analysis of India's BOP Position

Abstract :

The Balance of Payments (BOP) of a country reveals its financial and economic status which can be used as an indicator to determine whether the country's currency value is appreciating or depreciating. BOP records all transactions that create demand and supply of currency
It gives the government a broad perspective on a different range of import and export tariffs. The government then takes measures to increase and decrease the tax to discourage import and encourage export respectively and be self sufficient. BOP may indicate policy shift of the monetary authority (RBI)of the country

Key words:

Balance of payment, Balance of trade, Surplus, Deficit, Current account, Capital account, Disequilibrium

Introduction :

Balance of payment

Systematic record of all economic transaction between residents of a country and rest of the world in a given period of time in form of an accounting statement is known as balance of payments Residents of a country include individuals from government agencies. Those transactions which involve transfer of title or ownership of goods, services, money and assets are referred as economic transaction

It can broadly be categorised as under:

•visible items

•invisible items

•unilateral transfers

•capital transfers

Balance of Trade :

Difference between the amount of exports and imports of visible items (goods) is known as balance of trade

Balance of trade = exports of goods- imports of good

Credit (positive) side of BOP account records all export item whereas debit (negative) side of BOP account records all import items. It is not necessary that export of goods always equal to import of goods. In case exports are more than imports then it is known as surplus BOT and when import of goods exceeds the export of goods it is known as deficit BOT

Components of BOP:

Current Account:

Current account of BOP refers to an account which records all the transactions relating to export and import of goods and services and unilateral transfers during a given period of time. Components of current account are :

Credit items
Debit items
Net credit (credit – debit)

1.Visible trade
Export of good

Import of goods
Net export of goods
(balance of trade)

2.Invisible trade
Export of services

Import of goods
Net export of services

3.Uniletral transfers
Transfer receipt

Transfer payment
Net transfer receipts

4. Income receipt and payments
Income receipts

Income payment
Net income receipts

Current receipts(1+2+3+4)
Current payment
Current account balance

Capital Account :

Capital account of BOP refers to an account which records all the transactions between the residents of a country and the rest of world which can cause a change in assets or liabilities of the resident of a country or its government . componenets of capital account are :

Difference between current account and capital account :

Basis of difference
Current account
Capital account

Influence on economy
Current account transactions bring a change in the current level of a country's income

Capital account transactions bring about a change in the capital stock of a country

Concept

It is a slow concept as it includes all items of a flow nature

It is a stock concept as it includes all the items expressing changes in stock

Components

Current account = visible trade +invisible trade +unilateral transfer + income receipts and payment

Capital account= borrowing and lending to and from abroad + investments to another from abroad + change in foreign exchange reserves

India's Balance of Payment (BOP) crisis in 1991 :

Factors like the Gulf war and cumulative problems of the Indian economy led to BOP crisis in India in beginning of 1990s. India has been dependent on crude imports. International crude prices are very crucial for our BOP condition. When there was geopolitical disturbance due to Iraq crisis, crude prices shot up as did our import bill. Tourism dropped. It depleted our foreign exchange reserves. International rating agencies downgraded India. This fuelled the crisis further as India's credit worthiness plunged and there were no ready international lenders. A substantial outflow of deposits held by Non-resident

Indians during 1990–91 added to the crisis. Reserves declined to a low of $0.9 billion in January 1991. India had to pledge gold in May 1991 and again in July 1991 to avoid a default on its short-term debt servicing obligations. India borrowed foreign currency through India Development Bonds issued by the State Bank of India and Foreign Exchange Immunity Scheme of the Government of India. The scheme was aimed at attracting back the illegal foreign currency stashed abroad by resident Indians.

India came out of the crisis with an IMF-sponsored bail out. In course of time, Indian economy recovered, exports grew as rupee was devalued, foreign inflows started to pick up and we overcame the BOP pressures.

The rupee was devalued and brought closer to the market value as earlier it was artificially overvalued. International investors saw in this reform progress towards market orientation. Indian exporters felt encouraged as their earnings in foreign currency would fetch them more rupees. Devaluation was a precursor to rupee convertibility. Structural reforms were taken up so that the economy is put on a competitive path— opening the economy to globalization and so on.

Disequilibrium in BOP:

An imbalance created in balance of payment account due to increase in debit or credit of the account . the credit and debit side of the BOP account does not remain blanced always .

Disequilibrium of deficit arises when are receipts from the foreigner falls below our payment to foreigners it arises when the effective demand for given exchange of the country exceeds is it supply at a given rate of exchange this is called an unfavourable balance
Disequilibrium of surplus arises when the receipts of the country exceeds its payment such a situation arises when the effective demand for foreign exchange is less than supply such a surplus disequilibrium is terms as favourable balance

Causes of disequilibrium:
Economic factors
- developmental activities
- high rate of inflation
- cyclic flactuations
- change in demand
- import of sercices
Political factors
- political instability
- political disturbance
Social factors
- demonstration effect
- change in taste, prefrence, fashion and trends

Remedial measures of disequilibrium in BOP :

(i) Export promotion: Exports should be encouraged by granting various bounties to manufacturers and exporters. At the same time, imports should be discouraged by undertaking import substitution and imposing reasonable tariffs.

(ii) Import: Restrictions and Import Substitution are other measures of correcting disequilibrium.
(iii) Reducing inflation: Inflation (continuous rise in prices) discourages exports and encourages imports. Therefore, government should check inflation and lower the prices in the country.
(iv) Exchange control: Government should control foreign exchange by ordering all exporters to surrender their foreign exchange to the central bank and then ration out among licensed importers.
(v) Devaluation of domestic currency: It means fall in the external (exchange) value of domestic currency in terms of a unit of foreign exchange which makes domestic goods cheaper for the foreigners. Devaluation is done by a government order when a country has adopted a fixed exchange rate system. Care should be taken that devaluation should not cause rise in internal price level.

Statement of problem:

"“To analyse India's BOP position and identify the balance of current account and capital account along with overall balance of BOP account. "

Objectives:

To examine the performance of trade balance of Indian economy.
To analyze the status of indicators of balance of payments of economy of India.

Research Methodology :

The presented is based on descriptive research. Secondary Data has been collected from the various sources such as online publications, economic survey conducted by authorities, books. The data were taken for the period of 2016-2020. The result has been analysed using the graphs and charts predicting the status of balance of payments of Indian economy.

Literature Review :

Konya and Singh (2006) explained that export and import growth is very important for providing the base for economic growth in developing nations and international trade provides the link between output and growth.
Awokuse (2008) explored the total share of trade related to exports and imports for increasing the economic growth and concluded that export promotion contributes in the economic growth and development.
Athukorala (2011) examined the components of balance of payments Asian countries and China. The author showed that a nation with positive balance of trade and effective trade policy can increase the export performance and national output.

Data Analysis:

Net Import and Export of principal commodities:

Financial year

Exports (US $ Million)

Imports (US $ Million)

Trade balance (US $ Million)

2015-16

262291.1

381007.8

-118716.7

2016-17

275852.4

384357.0

-108504.6

2017-18

303526.2

465581.0

-162054.8

2018-19

330078.1

514078.4

-184000.3

2019-20

313361.0

474709.3

-163548.3

2020-21

291163.5

393610.6

-102447.1

The given graph represents the trade balance of principal commodities for the time period of 2015-2020 which are either imported or exported to and the from the country. Since 2015, imports have remained more than the exports till 2021. Imports had remain almost same around 380000 from 2015 to 2016 and then showed striking increase from around 380000 to 510000 in the year 2016-17 to 2018-19.the imports peaked at around 510000 in year 2018-19 and then started to fall till 2020-21. On the other hand exports had shown increase from 2015-16 to 2018-19 where it possessed its peak value of 330000 and the declined till 2020-21. In a nut shell, India had negative trade balance due to more of import then exports.

Current Account of BOP :

Financial year
Credit (Receipt)
Debit (Payment)
Net(surplus/deficit)

2015-16
501410
523560
-22151

2016-17
522189
536606
-14417

2017-18
592376

641093
-48717

2018-19
643719
700976
-57256

2019-20
642143
666799
-24656

2020-21
603553
579640
23912

The above graph represents net current account balance of BOP for a period of 2015-2020.the payment side of the current account had remained steady for 2 financial years and then showed constantly increased and peaked at around 640000 in the year 2018-19. Finally, the debit side declined for the next two consecutive years till 2021. Similarly, the receipt side of current account kept on increasing from 500000 to 640000 in the year 2015-16 to 2018-19 and remained constant for the year 2019-20. For the year 2020-21 the credit side of account slightly decreased to 600000. In a conclusion, current account had shown a net of deficit balance except the year 2020-21

Capital Account of BOP :

Financial year
Credit (Receipt)
Debit (Payment)
Net (surplus/deficit

2015-16
510058
468930
41128

2016-17
550649
514202
36447

2017-18
643612
552222
91390

2018-19
542482
488080
54403

2019-20
610038
526858
83180

2020-21
599025
535304
63721

The above graph represents net capital account of BOP for a period of 2015-2020. The payment side of the capital account has been increasing with a constant spend from 460000 to 550000 from the year 2015-16 to 2017-18. Then it had been fluctuating multiple times between 480000 and 530000. On other hand, receipt side of capital account has been increasing from year 2015-16 to 2017-18. Between 2017-18 to 2020-21 it had fluctuated many times between 540000 and 640000. Therefore, capital account had shown a net of surplus balance in the given period of time.

Overall Balance :

Financial year
Credit (Receipt)
Debit (Payment)
Net (surplus/deficit

2015-16
1011888
993984
17905

2016-17
1073215

1051665
21550

2017-18
1237887
1194313
43574

2018-19
1186784
1190123
-3339

2019-20
1254037
1194539
59498

2020-21
1203529
1116242
87286

The given graph represents overall balance of BOP for the time period of 2015-2020. The payment side and the receipt side of BOP account has almost shown the same amount and the maximum difference is 87000 in the financial year 2020-21. The payment side of the bop account first increased and then remained constant between 2017-2019. In the year 2020-21 it decreased to 1110000 whereas receipt side of BOP account first increased till the year 2017-18 and the fluctuated between 1180000 and 1250000. In a nut shell,BOP account had a surplus balance except the year 2018-19.

Conclusion :

Overall balance of payments is the sum of balance of current account and balance of capital account. It includes all the monetary transactions of the reporting country vis-a-vis rest of the world. A deficit in the current account must be settled by a surplus on the capital account.A surplus in the current account must be matched by a deficit on the capital account. The balance of payment must always balance in a book keeping sense. This is because for any surplus and deficit in the overall balance of payments there must be a corresponding debit or credit entry in the net changes in the external reserves. In other words, if there is a surplus it adds to external reserves of the country and is there is a deficit it reduces down the external reserves of the company

References :

Current account analysis

Net import and export of principal commodities is retrieved from the https://rbidocs.rbi.org.in/rdocs/Publications/PDFs/119TDD0650E8B3E0471F813FE9D7DFAEB827.PDFand

https://rbidocs.rbi.org.in/rdocs/Publications/PDFs/121T0BBF1A22C5404DDA9EBCFC6351E28560.PDF

Capital Account of Balance of Payment is retrieved from https://rbidocs.rbi.org.in/rdocs/Publications/PDFs/128T8F2B2130920547EFB8AB14D7C4A0A0B7.PDF

Current Account of Balance of Payment is retrieved from https://rbidocs.rbi.org.in/rdocs/Publications/PDFs/128T8F2B2130920547EFB8AB14D7C4A0A0B7.PDF

Overall Balance of Payment is retrieved from https://rbidocs.rbi.org.in/rdocs/Publications/PDFs/128T8F2B2130920547EFB8AB14D7C4A0A0B7.PDF

Changing Role of Banking

Mr. Ayan Jain
Author Bio: Author Mr. Ayan Jain, studying in class 11thof GD Goenka Public school , Delhi, has substantial interest in the subject economics .He strongly believes that country like India can develop by good economic strategies and methods.

Changing Role of Banking

ABSTRACT:

The banking institution plays an extremely crucial role in business development since they were brought to existence. The following study is conducted to mainly observe whether the banks are really playing an important role or not? Furthermore, the different types of services availed by businesses for a smooth functioning in day to day activities. The rate of interest involved at the time of borrowing a loan from bank and difficulties faced by businesses to get a credit. This study also involves many schemes that were implanted during the globalization privatization policy of 1991.These schemes helped and offered a opportunity to the banks as well as the businesses as both show a collateral relationship. This study also enlightens that in a country like India it is a necessity to encourage its citizen to shift towards a formal sector in terms of a financial society .

INTRODUCTION :

Economists have also defined a bank highlighting its various functions. According to Crowther, "The banker's business is to take the debts of other people to offer his own in exchange, and thereby create money." A similar definition has been given by Kent who defines a bank as "an organization whose principal operations are concerned with the accumulation of the temporarily idle money of the general public for the purpose of advancing to others for expenditure. banks are here to earn profits but it plays a very crucial role in development of aggregate or individual businesses.

The present study attempts to analyze that how much the business are aware of the banking norms and paperwork and what help do they seek from banking institution for their development.

Statements of Problem:

"To identify weather the banks are playing an important role in development of business".

OBJECTIVES:

To Identify that the businesses are aware about all

banking terminology?
To study that banking institution is important in functioning of business?
To identify that the electronic banking system is a useful methodology or not
To study that the business had taken a credit from bank or not ?
To identify that the businesses use the short-term credit facilities to meet their functioning or not?
To Identify that the businesses are satisfied with the credit rate provided by bank or not?
To study that that do the business think that banking institutions play an important role in building of Indian economy?

RESEARCH METHODOGY:

This study is based on primary data collected from general public through mailed questionnaire.
The period of the data is 4 months i.e. 11 may 2021to 11 September 2021
The study has been done on statistical methodology

LITERATURE REVIEW:

1-Sudhir Jain, Self-employed in his firm as a proprietor namely Sudhir Jain HUF and Ayan trading company since 2009,He is trading in steel aggregate raw material and an import export from Chinese markets .He maybe is well aware of all banking terminology and methodology his annual turnover is about 50,00,000 Indian rupees He well knowingly uses banking in his business ,he undoubtedly knows that banks are very important in development in his business although he has takes credit from his bank but he is not at all satisfied from the credit rate provided by his bank, lastly he also suggest that the government of India should take a measure or introduce a policy so that the rate of interest is minimized.

2- Adish Jain and Kamlesh Jain, working Directors in a public international company FNS INTERNATIONAL LTD. There annual income lies between 25,00,000-1,00,00,000. They are extremely well aware of all banking terminology and methodology they are working since the year 2005. they are in a manufacturing and retailing in high end luxury table ware and cutlery. They had taken credit and availed overdraft facilities from there bank as funds are require to meet business expansion but, pessimistically they are not at all satisfied with the credit rate provided by bank they are well aware the banks are required to develop small or aggregate businesses but they seek any solution to lower down the high amount of interest charged by bank and in return the current accounts in India are offered with very zero interest on deposits. additionally they also tell that the harsh paperwork demanded by bank is extremely painful.

Banking Sector Reforms from 1991:

The banking sector occupied a central place in the economic reforms and structural reforms that India conducted from 1991. The need arose due to deteriorating bank performance that was visible in:

• Lack of profitability.

• High Statutory Liquidity Ratio (SLR) and Cash Reserve Ratio (CRR).

• No credit discipline as there were loan melas when loans were liberally given without
any merit.

• Lack of competition as there were hardly any private domestic and foreign banks.

• Directed and concessional lending for populist reasons.

• Administered interest rates set by the RBI.

The reforms to set the above problems right were:

• Interest rates were deregulated to make banks respond dynamically to the market conditions. Even savings bank deposit rates were deregulated in 2011.

• Voluntary Retirement Scheme (VRS) for better work culture and productivity.

• Floor and cap on CRR were removed and floor on SLR was removed in 2006.

• Near level playing field for public, private and foreign banks in entry.

• Basel norms adopted for safe banking.

• FDI up to 74 per cent was permitted in private banks.

• Differentiated banking so as to cater to the unbanked and also leverage technology to
reach the unreached–for the last mile access to the remotely located.

• Bank consolidation through merger.

• Indradhanush comprising banking sector reforms for professionalization and strength.

The above reforms are meant to achieve the following objectives:

• To make banks competitive and profitable.

- To strengthen the sector to face global challenges.
- Sound and safe banking.
- To help banks technologically modernize for customer benefit.
- Make global expertise and capital available by relaxing FDI norms.
- Inclusive banking

Narasimham Committee [Under Finance minister Dr Manmohan singh]

8.1-Banking sector reforms in India were conducted on the basis of Narasimham Committee reports I and II (1991 and 1998 respectively), on the first report primarily.
The recommendations of Narasimham committee 1991 are:

- No more nationalization as we need to give confidence to domestic private and foreign investors.
- Create a level playing field between the public sector, private sector and foreign sector banks.
- Select few banks like SBI for global operations.
- Reduce Statutory Liquidity Ratio (SLR) and Cash Reserve Ratio (CRR) as that will leave more resources with banks for lending.
- Rationalize and better target priority sector lending as a sizeable portion of it is wasted and
also much of it is turning into non-performing assets (NPAs).
- Introduce prudential norms for better risk management and transparency in operations.
- Deregulate interest rates.

• Set up Asset Reconstruction Company (ARC) that can take over some of the bad debts off the banks and financial institutions and restructure them on profitable lines.

8.2-Most of these reforms are implemented:

• SLR and CRR are drastically reduced.

• Divestment in public sector banks led to their listing on the stock exchanges and their performance has improved.

• Private banks have been given licenses.

• SBI's associate banks have merged with SBI to scale up the operations.

• ARCs are functioning

Bank for International Settlements (BIS):

The Bank for International Settlements (BIS) is an international financial institution owned by central banks which 'fosters international monetary and financial cooperation and serves as a bank for central banks'. It also provides banking services, but only to central banks and other international organizations. It is based in Basel, Switzerland. There are 60 member central banks or monetary authorities in the BIS, including India.

Regulation (Amendment) Act 2017:

It amended the Banking Regulation Act, 1949 to allow RBI to issue directions to banks for initiating recovery proceedings against loan defaulters under the recently enacted Insolvency and Bankruptcy Code, 2016 (IBC). RBI acted on these powers and directed banks to initiate recovery proceedings against many defaulters.

Analysis, Interpretation and Presentation of data :
The data is examined with simple statistical tools like arithmetic mean, mode and median also the data is presented in form of pie diagram
Mean = , mode = most appearing value in series, median=center most value of series

AGE
This Pie-diagram shows that the maximum number of people engaged in a economic activity lies between 33-50 years of age and minimum lies above the age of fifteen and additionally
shifting towards an modern era we can see that the people below age of 18 are also engage in some start ups or business activities .

Gender

The following data shows that a greater number of females are involved in any kind of economic activity and also it displays India still deals with lots of stereotype against women.

State your profession
The following data shows that more than 90% of people are engage in business sector and less are employed or a government of India.

Annual income
This pie diagram shows us that mostly people have an

income around 1,00,000-10,00,000 and equal amount people have income between 10 lakh to 1 crore.

Do you believe that banks play a crucial role in business development?
This data shows us that every unit of population believe that the banking institutions plays and crucial role in business development.

If you are businessman ,you are a:-

This data tells us that most of the business enterprises are engaged in manufacturing activities and the amount of least people is in retail sector of business.

Do you use e banking services in your business?
This data tells us that more than 90% of people use electronic banking methodology in there day to day business activities and there is a quite a few number of people who do not use e banking services.

When you think about banking so do you think that is important in business?

Do you think that Banking is important in a business?
The following pie diagram shows us that the approximately 91.30% of public assures that the banking institutions are required as well as important in business at each possible time and rest of less than 9% thinks denies the following statement. Reasons can be many like lack of educational

knowledge, etc.

Are you aware of all banking terminology?
The pie diagram presents the fact that more than 60% of people are extremely well aware of banking terminology and a quite number of people approximately 17.40% are not at all aware of banking terminology and tentative replies are received from around 21.70% public that are not extremely sure about the terms but a rough sketch do come to their mind.

How would you rate electronic banking services?

The following data displays its readers that the more than 65% people replies that they find the e services to be saving but on the other hand around 8.7% people thinks or personally have some fear of theft as online world is not what is seem to.

From which type of banks would you rather prefer to avail service?
The collected shows us that more population to avail services from public sector bank might be many reasons like now days, many private sector financial institutions are getting insolvent due to embezzlement of public funds or etc.

Have you ever taken credit/loan from your bank?
the following data represents that more than 69% of total population had ever taken credit from their bank but on the other hand there many who don't know about credit sector of bank and many had not ever taken.

Have you ever used overdraft facilities provided by your bank?
The pie chart shows us that approx. 50% of population had used overdrafts in their as they are extremely crucial as business do not have surplus funds at times so these services are used but now also around half of population isn't aware of overdrafts or not used.

Are you satisfied with credit/interest rate provided by the bank?
This following pie diagram tells us that amount of the population satisfied with the credit rate provided by the banks thus, we can observe that not even 50% of total are satisfied and quite low people are satisfied with the credit rate.

Do you think that banking is required in smooth functioning of Indian economy?
The pie diagram explains the fact that around 87% of the population believes in the statement, according to their own opinion that positively banking institutions do help is smooth functioning of an economy but approximately 13% of population affirms a negative reply for the following statement.

Conclusion:

The following study is examined and finally concludes the following:-
In a county like India where the majority of its population

deals or come from an informal sector in terms of money so, accordingly the banking institution are playing an important role but the general public are still finding some or another difficulty in either paperwork levied by the banks or in not getting appropriate rate of interest also, the fact is that India stills deals with an uneducated population and that is one of the biggest reason of an emerging informal sector of credits and deposits.By this, the following study is concluded but at last the government of India should plan a scheme to reduce the rate of interest on deposits as well as credits and lower the % of tax liabilities so that a shift from informal to formal sector could be possible in near future.

Human Capital Shifts and Sectoral Development with Special Emphasis on Industry Specific Innovation A Behavioural Economics Perspective

Mr. Samarth Sarthak Shandilya

Author Bio: Mr. Samarth Shandilya, a 12th grade student, recently pursuing academic internship with Dr.Manoj Kumar, Assistant professor of international relations at Delhi University. His approaches global migration and human capital shifts with an interdisciplinary lens, focusing on behavioural economics and innovation.

Human capital shifts and sectoral development with special emphasis on industry specific innovation: A behavioural economics perspective.

ABSTRACT:

Shift of human capital has existed from time immemorial, the complex factors facilitating it and consequent motivations that have a dynamic interplay has however changed with time. The main purpose of this research paper is to analyse this diverse component of population change. This will be done by analyzing the following, first, the primary question of "why migration?" through a fundamental difference between the Human capital theories and the concepts of behavioural economics to increase our understanding of 'predictable irrationals' such as driving factors, loss aversion, risk seeking & passions. Secondly, examining the impact of the global shift in human capital promoting sectoral development of certain industries with special emphasis on the technology industry. Finally, examining the complex interaction between industry specific innovation and economic development instigated by human capital shifts. The idea of human-uniqueness and behavioural unpredictability will help us extend the classical economic concepts to analyse and forecast migration and at the same time help us device a hypothesis (cited in the paper) that can be used for quantifiable human capital data in real life as we understand the difference between human capital and production outcomes.

INTRODUCTION :

Throughout the history of humanity, every once in a while, things change dramatically that make the entire functioning of the various complex elements of our life function differently. This change seems so subtle that it is only observed in retrospect. This changing context of our lives, according to me, can be classified into different ages or eras.

Broadly recognising the major eras, the classification according to me is as follows- First, the age of land operations, followed by the age of bricks and roads, the age of construction and as trade developed, we observed the emergence of the age of machines (physical forms of technology) then to an age of pure technology, which is the age of today. I believe that humanity is now on the cusp of a new era, a new age of human capital, where humans and tech enabled human capital terminate the difference between the consumers and producers. Then perhaps, the futuristic portrayal of technology becoming the enabler of human capital might not be that distant. My point is that this change, in the importance of human capital, is something that is very important to understand and study. An era where creativity and design is of immense value. The future is definitely a challenge to the status quo.

A fact that has transcended time is that humans are migratory by nature. As we dive into understanding this concept in a more elaborate way, it is crucial for us to understand the unconscious behavioural tendencies that cause migration. Furthermore, As this new era of human capital employs more importance to the granular understanding of each individual, it is important for us to recognise the migration of human capital and its pattern in certain sectors and industries and the possible motivations that attract individual aspirations from throughout the world.

Subsequently emphasising on market/industry influence of the same that runs corresponding to this-deemed-new era of technology enabled human capital, where the growth of human capital runs parallel to the deceleration of importance of physical capital and technological investments, which is ironically, in the very same era of technology-indicating the change that is ongoing right now.

It is without a doubt very crucial for us to analyse these global changes in a way that it does not reduce humans to mere blocks of data, rather analysing this change at a 'human level' that will help us to devise a realistic critique towards the already applied uses of human capital data and assessment.

As we progress further in this paper, we aim not to delve into whether this migration should take place or not, instead, the paper aims at understanding how to regulate this change in a way that maintains the economic and social equilibrium of the world is more practical. One way to optimise this regulation is through the concept of CARE -Creation, Attraction, Retention and Ability to enable human capital, given by Dr. Constantin Gurdgiev.

Study :

1. Behavioural economic insight on migration theories and human capital migration.

One of the biggest mistakes done by erstwhile economic migration theorists is to assume humans as rational and selfish and/or self-interested individuals, most of these theories being based on the view of neoclassical and classical economics. The problem with this model is that it is very unrealistic in its application, and this narrative has been recently widely recognised and accepted since the school of thought of behavioural economics has been on the rise. The truth is humans are irrational, often selfless and almost always affected by social factors and preferences. Factors such as happiness, social preferences, personal characteristics, gains vs. losses, loss aversion and risk aversion, risk-seeking and endowment effect among many others are exactly the type of variables that are necessary to extend the neoclassical theories to make it more practical. Reduction of assumptions on standard economics models could achieve more reality reflecting explanations of human behaviour causing migration.

Standard economics view of migrations:

The fundamental model of neoclassical theory highlights that migration is a result of interregional wage differentials, distance between origin and destination, and labor market conditions such as the unemployment rate and market fluctuations as factors determining migration.The formative work of Sjaastad'sHuman Capital Theory (1962)provides a theoretical framework for examining households' decisions to relocate from a geographical area, defining the issue as their desire to maximise their net economic return on human capital.

Some of the other major neoclassical theories are : Smith (1776) and Ravenstein's (1889) Economic Equilibrium Theory, Heckscher (1949) and Ohlin's (1993)
Migration Theory, Todaro (1969) and Harris-Todaro's (1970) Rural-Urban Migration Theory, Lee's (1966) Early Decision-Making Theory, Borjas' (1987) Self-Selection Theory, and Piore's (1979) Dual Labour Market Theory.

Recent analysis of other factors :

The neoclassical view has been subject to justified criticism as it is "viewed as mechanically reducing migration determinants, ignoring market imperfections, homogenising migrants and migrant societies and being ahistorical and static" (Kurekova, 2011, p.7).

This study of recentlyanalyzed migration variables are proposed by various authors who extend the theories of new economics. These include Bonasiaand Napolitano (2012), Cattaneo (2008), Czaika and Vothknecht (2014), Czaika (2015), Jennissen (2004), Kurunova (2013), Polgreen and Simpson (2011), Tupa and Strunz (2013), Van der Gaag and Van Wissen (2008). The factors recognised by these theories have been summarised in table 1.1 (Dr InetaŽičkutė, 2015).

Some key ideas of economic human behaviour that are the hallmark contradictions to classical theories are:

- The availability heuristic refers to the idea that people often rely on easily recalled information, rather than actual data.
- Bounded rationality refers to the fact that people have limited cognitive information, ability and time, and do not always make the "correct" choice that is often anticipated from an economist's point of view.
- Bounded self-interest is the idea that people are often willing to choose a less beneficial outcome for themselves if it means they can support others.
- Bounded willpower captures the idea that people are not patient and often choose short term benefits over an optimal choice.

- Loss aversion is the idea that people are more averse to losses than they are eager to make gains.

It is true that these behavioural tendencies are universal in nature and give a rather needed insight towards the human capital shift argument. From the above observation of new variables, we will have a better insight towards the shift of human capital as a process fuelled not only by purely economic and logical decisions, but also factors such as loss aversion, bounded rationality, bounded willpower, social preferences and passions; characteristics that inevitably "human". Traditional factors analysis based onstandard economics explanations should be reconsidered with behavioural factors insights, trying to answer questions such as how are common passions, such as, greater moral understanding of life showcasing patterns of shift of human capital migration from advanced economies to developing economies, or vice- versa. How are the factors of loss aversion being observed in scepticism faced by subjects prone to inter-regional migration?

2. Economic development in the age of human capital.

It is considered irrefutable that human capital accumulation corresponds to increase in economic development of a region. Globalization and economic integration have changed lifestyles and impacted consumption patterns and preferences, which in turn has changed production patterns all over the world and instigated FDIs that indirectly also run parallel to human capital shifts. In this sense the road of economic

development and human capital runs two-ways, where either of the two factors could cause the emergence of the other.
Another phenomenon in action is the connection between innovation of industries and economic development. It has been observed that as the accumulations of human capital integrate with high productivity levels the innovation levels of that said industry also increases hence causing economic development of the region. One important sector that acts as a flag bearer of this phenomenon is the pure technology sector, where, since the past decade, the leading companies have been creating a Mecca for highly skilled technological intensive human capital migration; examples of this are -- San Francisco and California-- the growing technological hubs of the world.

This can be observed via analysing whether there are persisting effects of human capital on innovation and economic development using regional historical human capital and current innovation and economic development data and the observation of the said innovation development can be done through the study of industry-specific patent study (Pellegrino, Gabriele and Penner, Orion B. and Piguet, Etienne and de Rassenfosse, Gaétan, Immigration and Inventor Productivity (October 24, 2019)).

But as we understand this complex connection, it is important to note that high human capital does not correspond to high productivity. This is often a very inaccurate assumption made. Harvard economist Richard Freeman, argued that human capital only acted as a signal about talent and ability; real productivity came later through training, motivation, and capital equipment. He concluded that human capital should not be considered a factor of production. Production levels often more closely relate to the work environment along with human capital. Achievement scores in various growth models are testimony to this intricate relation. Again, correlating to the technology industry hub, perhaps this method of retaining portable human capital along with providing appropriate work environment factors (such as working hours, human capital levels of other workers and physical capital etc) lead to higher achievement scores.

Perhaps this methodology of quantifying the achievement scores objectively will be a groundbreaking advancement for the evaluation of human capital scores that correspond more closely to production levels and real world application of human capital scores in a way that is more realistic to real world work foundations and structures.

To achieve this remarkable feat it is also important to create ways to evaluate human capital that justify the gradual evolution of education, especially keeping in mind the covid-education reform, new subjective ways such as emphasising more on 'quality' of education rather than quantity. Such changes will construct a new narrative of human capital that does justice to the contemporary interpretations of novel work and requirements of the increasingly competitive industry growth.

CONCLUSION:

It seems most likely that the behavioural economical factors are the key to make the interpretation of neoclassical and new economic migration theories more accurate with the aim to reason the human capital shift globally. Perhaps, future studies and research in this area will make it easy for institutions, nations and individuals to forecast brain drain and human capital shifts and will give the ability to tailor appropriate migration regulations and developmental strategies to alleviate area-specific sectoral growth.

It is fair to say that it is universally accepted now, that there is a very dynamic interplay between human capital accumulation and economic growth. Both of these factors can trigger the onset of each other.

It is also true that the same complex relationship exists between economic growth and innovation, where both these factors work in a cordial way. Furthermore, human capital shifts also promote economic growth along with higher innovation probability as the migrated skilled workers showcase higher productivity levels (Immigration and Inventor Productivity (October 24, 2019)).

As the world changes, we better our understanding of the complex functioning of humanity way beyond numbers and statistics. It is time that we recognise the intricate relation between human capital and productivity scores academically. Subsequently, productivity level fluctuations act as a direct factor in affecting the achievement scores. It is hopeful that these achievement scores can be implied in novel ways in the near future to make the application of human capital in pace with the developmental levels of the current age.

REFERENCES:

Constant in Gurdgiev - lecture on Human Capital and Age of Change

Kooiman, N., Latten, J. and Bontje, M. (2018), Human Capital Migration: A Longitudinal Perspective. Tijds. voor Econ. en Soc. Geog, 109: 644-660. https://doi.org/10.1111/tesg.12324
Erik Angner, George Loewenstein,

Behavioral Economics,
Philosophy of Economics, North-Holland, 2012, https://doi.org/10.1016/B978-0-444-51676-3.50022-1.

(https://www.sciencedirect.com/science/article/pii/B978 0444516763500221)

Žičkutė, Ineta&Kumpikaite, Vilmante. (2015). Theoretical Insights on the Migration Process from Economic Behaviour's Perspective. Procedia - Social and Behavioral Sciences. 213. 873-878. 10.1016/j.sbspro.2015.11.498.

Dr Alain Samson (2014), An Introduction to Behavioral Economics

https://www.behavioraleconomics.com/resources/introd

uction-behavioral-economics/

Pellegrino, Gabriele and Penner, Orion B. and Piguet, Etienne and de Rassenfosse, Gaétan, Immigration and Inventor Productivity (October 24, 2019)
Reenen, John. (2011). Human resource management and productivity.

Economic Migration, Networks and Human Capital Transferability from the New European Borderlands By Alexander M. Danzer*, Barbara Dietz -

https://www.econstor.eu/obitstream/10419/39903/1/AEL_2008_7_danzer.pdf

Sustainable Development A Peace Policy of Future

Ms. Saniya Gupta
Author Bio: Ms.Saniya Gupta , class 12th grader of G.D. Goenka , is playing an active part in advocating , implementing and championing Sustainable Development Goals through collaborative efforts.

Sustainable Development: A peace policy of future

"Sustainable Development is the peace policy of future"
-Dr. Klaus Topfër

What is Sustainable Development?

Sustainable development can be defined as development that meets the needs of the present without compromising the ability of future generations to meet their own needs. In other words, as the name suggests, fulfilling the presents needs and wants without exploiting the resources for future is known as sustainable development.

Sustainable development in India :

India, is the second most populated country of the world with alarming and unequal literacy-poverty rates and sex ratio. With existing unequal distribution of resources, pollution far more than permissible levels, red-tapism, corruption and age old toxic traditions like sati system, parda system, dowry, female infanticide ,etc. it is very important for the government and citizens of India to adapt a sustainable approach, to combat the problems of the ever growing illiterate population.
Statistics state that Top 10% of the Indian population holds more than 77% of national income leaving our nation clasped in the dungeons of poverty and slavery.

The sex ratio may have become better through the ages but not the conditions of the females .
To state it otherwise now actually more percentage has to suffer the brutally unethical and uneducated society. Apart from people the animals and environment is also in ruins.The contaminated River Yamuna never fails to secure our nation major headlines in international news! What a glory,isn't it?

India-the land of toxic rivers and notions.

And the people? All what we do is blame the political leaders and like the instagram-twitter posts where they're criticised by the opposition. For how long shall the corroded Golden Bird survive with each of its realm ashen with contagious ignorance and indifference?

International measures taken:

The Sustainable Development Goals or Global Goals are a collection of 17 interlinked global goals designed to be a "blueprint to achieve a better and more sustainable future for all". The SDGs were set up in 2015 by the United Nations General Assembly and are intended to be achieved by the year 2030.

The 17 sustainable development goals (SDGs) to transform our world:

GOAL 1: No Poverty
GOAL 2: Zero Hunger
GOAL 3: Good Health and Well-being
GOAL 4: Quality Education
GOAL 5: Gender Equality
GOAL 6: Clean Water and Sanitation
GOAL 7: Affordable and Clean Energy
GOAL 8: Decent Work and Economic Growth
GOAL 9: Industry, Innovation and Infrastructure
GOAL 10: Reduced Inequality
GOAL 11: Sustainable Cities and Communities
GOAL 12: Responsible Consumption and Production
GOAL 13: Climate Action
GOAL 14: Life Below Water
GOAL 15: Life on Land
GOAL 16: Peace and Justice Strong Institutions
GOAL 17: Partnerships to achieve the Goal

Measures by Indian Government :

In 2015, the United Nations established the 2030 Agenda for Sustainable Development with 17 identified SDGs to help UN member states achieve inclusive, people-centred and holistic development together. The NITI Aayog launched the first edition of its index in 2018 to monitor the country's progress on the goals through data-driven assessment, and to encourage the States and Union Territories in achieving them.

NITI Aayog's latest SDG India Index states that India has made steady progress towards achieving the United Nations' Sustainable Development Goals in areas of health, energy, and infrastructure. Further, India's overall score across SDGs improved by 6 points; from 60 in 2019 to 66 in 2020-21 with nation-wide improvement in 'clean water and sanitation' and 'affordable and clean energy'. The third edition of the Index highlighted the significance of partnerships in achieving the larger 2030 Agenda. Indian states of Kerala, Himachal Pradesh, Tamil Nadu, Andhra Pradesh and Goa have achieved much better indexes than the previous years

Global Appeal:

The environment doesn't discriminate between people and nations. It's effect is common to all! Before the collision and diversion of tectonic plates, our world was also geographically one.
it is our responsibility to look after our global community. all countries are mutually co-existing and fulfilling each other's needs and wants, for example of India is deficit of petroleum, it will import it from Arab countries, similarly all the countries and co-existing.
Nature had blessed humans with a perfectly self sufficient

eco-system which replenished food, life, water and nitrogen through its own ecological cycles but with construction of concrete roads leading to hindrance in water seepage, excessive gap between haves and have nots, corruption, increase in population, contamination etc. the whole cycle disrupted. On one hand we have rich business men wasting tons of food after elaborate parties while poor starving for a basic meal on the other.

Changing the world in a whole is a nightmare while if each individual looks after their immediate surroundings, the adverse situation can be made a 100 times better in the shortest passage of time. Just a few acts of kindness and a few conscious and deliberate efforts can make the world a better place for our upcoming generations . Making basic changes in mentality and lifestyle to encourage cleanliness and social betterment is important not only for future needs but also for the present quality of life.

Together, We can and we will as we must

Some small changes that can be adopted by people of all ages and levels:

1. Educate your house help.
2. organise cleaning drives in your locality monthly or just take charge of your immediate surroundings.
3. Fix leaking faucets.
4. Turn the tap off while brushing.
5. Use bucket for bathing ,washing cars and watering the plants instead of shower and pipe.
6. Don't waste food and distribute the excess instead of throwing away.

7. Feed the stray animals of your locality in turns
8. Install chimneys
9. Car pool
10. Plant trees
11. Turn off engines on red lights
12. Don't burst crackers on any occasion
13. Eliminate the usage of plastic
14. Use recyclable items
15. Turn off lights and switches when not in use
16. Use handkerchiefs instead of tissue paper
17. Use soap bars instead of plastic bottles
18. Reuse or repurpose old clothes
19. Reduce your carbon footprint
20. Hang dry clothes instead of driers
21. Stop teaching boys that "boys don't cry"
22. Stop expecting that girls shall only be house keepers
23. Encourage labour and illiterate around you to go for deriving basic education or teach them by yourself.
24. Discourage child labour
25. Support local handicraft to eliminate poverty
26. Install solar panels in offices and buildings
27. Get regular pollution check for vehicles
28. Sit for sunlight in an hour and save electricity
29. Distribute sanitary pads, sanitisers and masks to the underprivileged
30. Contribute 1-2 books each to
31. set up a library for your locality

Conclusion:

For our current and future generations to have happy and

long lives and for the biosphere to have a healthy balance it is our duty to maintain a clean,safe,educated and sustainable environment. We can't leave our basic responsibilities in the hands of just the government and legislature, not only through policies and programs but also through small changes, efforts and awareness it's important for each one of us to answer the wake up call of the collapsing world.

Who would if we won't?

Only Man, the social animal has the capacity to protect or destroy the ecosystem common to all marine and terrestrial creatures. We can't let this beautiful gift of nature turn into a chaotic mess just to fulfil our selfish motive .

Harnessing River Health

Ms. Ishanvie Bansal

Author Bio: Ms. Ishanvie Bansal is a responsible student of a reputed school in Delhi, India with eight years of experiènce in Debating and Public Speaking with various recognized institutions. Ishanviespecializes in administration and is a young entrepreneur of a home-based bakery. She is a powerful force in the workplace and uses her positive attitude and tireless energy to encourage her employees and the people around her. She is inspired daily by her mother and her aunts. In her free time, Ishanvie likes to read to her grandmother.

Harnessing River Health

Imagine the sight of you taking a dip in the holiest river of India, the Ganga, to attain purity and forgiveness and coming out to a fleet of floating corpses, possibly covid contaminated. Yes, this has happened. Unfortunate yet happening. Further imagine being surrounded with heaps of plastic waste and remains of idols. Gruesome, isn't it?
Water is life matter and matrix, mother and medium. There is no life without water.Ganga is one of the most polluted rivers in the world with contamination levels

3,000 times higher than prescribed by the WHO. It's heart rendering to watch people avidly contribute to the destruction of the water bodies either through their malicious plastic dumping or their prestigious ritual of idol immersion or even illegally immersing corpses. These often-overlooked detrimental polluters are comprising every ounce of water's purity and eventually the survival of future generations to come.

The harms caused to the water bodies are hideous. Plastic indeed has revolutionized the world but has extensively impacted water bodies. Every year, we produce 300 million tons of plastic waste. That's nearly equivalent to the weight of the entire human population. We are literally sitting in a plastic time bomb.

Adding to this evil is the problem of idol immersion. All that glitters is not gold. Almost one lakh idols made of plaster of Paris (POP), toxic paints and hazardous chemicals (calcium sulphate hemihydrate) are immersed after festivities like Ganesh Chaturthi and Durga puja and affect water's purity for nearly a century, adding not only to the adulterations but also creating waterborne diseases.

Forget the future; do we even have enough resources to survive the present? While the solution to this self-advanced jeopardy stands right before us, all it requires is an effort to maintain the quality of life that the water bodies have provided to humankind, while sustaining the integrity of their ecosystems. Let's follow the 4 R's (Reduce, Reuse, Recycle, Recover) because the future is all ours.

Let us avoid using products that contain micro beads. Usage of everything biodegradable – from foods to detergents to sanitary pads made from bamboo, cotton, tree peel, and the like must be practically done.

Social entrepreneurs like Harinder Singh Kukreja and many others have already come up with sustainable alternatives like chocolate Ganesha. We must encourage people to make such eco-friendly switches to alum, cow dung, turmeric or neem leaves made idols holding water purifying properties; idols which can serve as feed for aquatic life; plantable idols made of vermin compost or seed of fast-growing plants or edible fruit idols. Organizing social media campaigns and physical stall setups selling eco-friendly idols at subsidized rates can be the most effective measures in this regard.

Moreover, residents of a locality with active involvement of the youth, can organize 'clean water campaigns' on a fortnightly basis to clean local water bodies surrounding them. Human well-being cannot be achieved without the protection and conservation of the Earth's ecosystem.

"When We Heal the Earth, We Heal Ourselves"

Analysis of India's Marital Status on Labour Comparison

Ms. Mehak Malhotra

Author Bio: Author Ms. Mehak Malhotra is a student Researcher, immensely passionate about writing. Her keen interests lie in Economics, Environment, Human Rights especially women empowerment, LGBTQ.
She is an avid Badminton player and actively participates in Dance and Dramatics. She is an incoming freshman at New York University, majoring in Economics and fashion.

Analysis of India's Marital Status on Labour Comparison

Abstract:

Globally, women living with a partner, in most cases married to a man, are less likely to be in the labour force than women living alone, although they have higher-than-average labour force participation rates. Most worryingly, India is losing its most educated and productive women. National Sample Survey (NSS) data shows that women who have passed higher secondary have the lowest female labour force participation in India. This is to say nothing of the 'marriage penalty' or 'child penalty' for women who drop out of the labour force due to marriage and childbirth. It is increasingly obvious that standard economic theory has it exactly backwards. We can't wait for incomes to rise incomes in India will stagnate unless we find ways to get women, especially the most economically productive, back into the labour force. This paper tries to analyse and identify the India's Marital Status on Labour Comparison.

Key Words:

Married, unmarried, equality, opportunities, impact, paid, work firm, women, men

Introduction:

Around the world, active engagement in the labour force is the key through which people earn a living. It is one of the main ways through which individuals can have an independent source of income, and it is an essential means through which people ensure decent living conditions for themselves and their families. Paid work provides a path towards economic independence, overall well-being, human dignity, and self-actualization. Women and men both rely on these opportunities to care for and sustain their families.

Equal opportunity and the equal treatment in the labour market are the main aspects of sustainable development.

But does everyone in society have the same access to decent work? Do women and men have the same opportunities? What is the impact of discriminatory social norms and gender stereotypes on women's labour force participation? To what extent is the participation of women and men linked to their family situation?

Until recently, a reliable data needed to explore the links between gender gaps in labour force participation, marital status that the decision to work outside the home is usually a household decision, i.e., women living with a partner, in most cases married to a man, are less likely to be in the labour force.

Although they have higher-than-average labour force participation rates Most worryingly, India is losing its most educated and productive women. This is to say nothing of the 'marriage penalty' or 'child penalty' for women who drop out of the labour force due to marriage and childbirth. It is increasingly obvious that standard economic theory has it exactly backwards. We can't wait for incomes to rise.

Incomes in India will stagnate unless we find ways to get women, especially the most economically productive, back into the labour force.

STATEMENT OF THE PROBLEM:

"To analyse India's Marital Status on Labour Comparison and to examine the Equal treatment in the labour market"

Objectives:

1. To study the India's Marital Status on Labour Comparison
2. To analyse the Equal treatment in the labour market
3. To examine is the impact of discriminatory social norms and gender stereotypes on women's labour force participation.

Research Methodology :

The presented is based on descriptive research. Primary Data (in the form of questionnaire) has been collected from the various sources such as online publications, economic survey conducted by authorities, books. The data were taken for the period of 2015-2021. The result has been analysed using the graphs and charts predicting the Marital Status on Labour Comparison.

Literature Review:

Jyotirmoy Bhattacharya, who teaches economics at Ambedkar University offers an explanation that there are enough anecdotal accounts of women being forced to quit their jobs after getting married or giving birth to a child.Married men are more likely to participate in the labour force, more preferred by employers and earn more their unmarried counterparts. Whereas for women, studies found that it is the unmarried women who participate more in the labour market, get employed and earn more than married women.

The researchers, Professor Hema Swaminathan and Professor Deepak Malghan, of the Centre for Public Policy, Indian Institute of Management in Bangalore, used data from 2.85 million households made up of heterosexual couples between the ages of 18 and 65 years. The most recent wave of data suggests that when both members of the couple are employed, there is not a single place, not even in the richest or most developed parts, where wives earn as much as their husbands. A woman's lower income can have consequences beyond the economic, the researchers say, affecting gender dynamics in the household and putting women at a disadvantage.

Data Analysis:

Chart 1:

According to the paid leave force, Every employee shall be paid for the period of his leave at a rate equivalent to the daily average of his wages for the days on which he actually worked during the preceding three months, exclusive of any earnings in respect of overtime but inclusive of dearness allowance. In the following pie chart (chart 1), we can clearly see that 59.4 percent of people think that married women are provided with paid home leaves but most of them are married men as compared to married women. While 25 percent of the people think that married women are not provided with paid leaves and most of them are married women as compared to married men.

Chart 2:

In the following pie chart2, we can observe that 50 percent of the people think that women are not paid less than men, while most of them are men and 37.5 percent of the people think that women are paid less than men and most of them are females. As a result, there's a lifetime of income inequality between men and women and more women are retiring into poverty.

Chart 3:

In India, the top three job opportunities sought by both men and women are job security, a job that they love, and good work-life balance. While job security is critical for working women across India, women are laying more emphasis on the type of employer they choose to work with, the recognition they will receive for the work they do, and on the skills that will be utilised on the job. But despite having similar goals still women don't get fair opportunities at work. According to the pie chart 50 percent of the people who are women think that they don't get fair opportunities at work, while 34.4 percent of the people who are men think that women get fair opportunities.

Chart 4:

The above picture shows that a questionnaire was forwarded to the people who are working or have retired and were asked a question if they would prefer a married women working or an unmarried women working in a work firm, and we received different answers from different people, Few people said that the marital status of a woman does not determine her efficiency at work, just in the way a man's marital status does not determine his efficiency. Work output is based on the comfort with which the employees can be facilitated to work, not whether they can be exploited according to their marital status, while others said that women will pay less attention to work at the workplace as domestic responsibilities will take up their time after marriage. The norm also dictates that women make more 'compromises' after marriage – moving cities, changing jobs, settling for a less fulfilling job, or giving up working completely. companies view women as flaky employees who are less likely to stick around, especially once they break the news of marriage.

Conclusion:

Marriage is seen as a deterrent in a woman's career, which it can be, in the wrong organisation. This unconscious bias is dangerous, especially for unmarried women in leadership positions in the workplace, it is clear that in many cases, women's status in the workplace is largely determined by her personal life. This experience of sexism is common but isn't necessarily rampant. With more youth entering the market with their start-ups, with younger leaders taking over, and with existing hierarchies dissolving, there's a larger scope for an egalitarian outlook to prevail. The marital status of a woman does not determine her efficiency at work, just in the way a man's marital status does not determine his efficiency.

Work output is based on the comfort with which the employees can be facilitated to work, not whether they can be exploited according to their marital status .A strong solution identifies the root cause of the problem- the patriarchal mindset around the marriage and women. When organisations and leaders accommodate women and their needs, change can happen. When organisations and leaders accommodate women and their needs, change can happen. And if nothing else, calling it out can do itself too- "why do you say that?" "what did you mean by that?" can bring unconscious bias to the table. The workforce is gradually changing – women are climbing to the top and making their mark in industries far and wide. But we still have a long way to go, and structural changes are imperative.

REFERENCE:

Impact of Marital Status on Labour Comparison: https://docs.google.com/forms/d/e/1FAIpQLSdhiO6tVgLDJ8EExt09UNYYanbiUyQ5GFJF-3v2f4idDN-MUQ/viewform

THE IMPACT OF MARRIAGE AND CHILDREN ON LABOUR MARKET PARTICIPATION:https://sustainabledevelopment.un.org/content/documents/2701theimpactofmarriageandchildrenonlabourmarketparticipationen.pdf

Women and Work in India: https://www.hks.harvard.edu/sites/default/files/centers/cid/files/publications/faculty-working-

papers/women_work_india_cidwp339.pdf
Why are fewer Married Women Joining the Work Force in India:https://ftp.iza.org/dp9722.pdf
Unpaid_care_work.pdf:
https://www.oecd.org/dev/development-gender/Unpaid_care_work.pdf

Why Lesser Number Of Women Work Than Men

Ms. Tanisha Poddar

Author Bio : The author, Ms. Tanisha Poddar, is a high school student who is immensely passionate about writing and aims to be an entrepreneur. Being creative and spirited, she likes to voice her opinions and look at things from a unique perspective. She regularly posts blogs and has written other research papers mainly focusing about women in business.

Why Lesser Number Of Women Work Than Men?

ABSTRACT:

Gender equality is an important development objective in and of itself. Women globally have come a long way to accomplish and establish an equal position in the patriarchal society, still there remains a wide gap and liberating women professionally is important in order to overcome it. Increasing the number of women in work increases their agency and voice as well as boosts country's economic growth, leading to better productivity and improving prospects for future generations. Despite of this, less than 30% of working-age women are currently in work compared to nearly 80% of men in India. This paper focuses on the reasons behind the falling back of women in economic professions and provide ways to cope with it.

INTRODUCTION:

Women covers almost half the population in India and holds utmost importance in the functioning of nation as well as the world. It is important for both men and women to work and prosper for this world to reach a whole new level of success but sadly men have dominated this work-life cycle being entitled as the 'breadwinners' and leaving behind women for household chores. Even in twenty-first century, the current global labour force participation rate for women is close to 49%. For men, it's 75%. That's a difference of 26 percentage points, with some regions facing a gap of more than 50 percentage points. Women's position though have improved in the workforce but their progress over the past 10 years has not meant greater access to quality jobs, nor has it brought an end to discrimination especially in India. There still exists barriers which are holding women back in work and only a little is being done to eradicate it.

STATEMENT PROBLEM:

'Why lesser number of women work in comparison to men' +.

OBJECTIVES :

1. To study the reasons for large gender divide in Indian workforce.
2. To analyse the result of economic survey conducted.
3. To state possible solutions to overcome the problem.

HYPOTHESIS:

1. Gender discrimination still prevails in workforce which eludes women from getting equal opportunities as men.
2. Existence of socio-cultural barriers that do not let women earn.
3. Non- existence of safe and suitable working environment which keeps women behind.

LITERATURE REVIEW:

Number of studies has addressed this issue in different perspectives. Some of the papers related to this subject are reviewed.

Susan et al (1998) have focused on the work place gender discrimination rational bias theory. According to which, decision makers may choose to discriminate if they believe that their superiors or others having power over their careers expect or prefer it. The findings showed that businessmen discriminated women and people at the top of the organization are most biased against women than people at the bottom. Their study has also confirmed that management support discrimination, though those discriminations were less than the findings of earlier research, reflecting increasing equal opportunity. It was also confirmed through their research that the discrimination is more because of external pressures than from internal.

Wayne (1995) says that no law has ever attempted to define precisely the term' discrimination', in the context of workforce, it can be defined as the giving of an unfair advantage (or disadvantage) to the members of the particular group in comparison to the members of other group.

Uzma (2004) found out that an identity is created through the society, environment and parents. It is a two-way process - how people view you and how you view yourself. Parents usually consider their daughters as weak, timid, and too vulnerable; they need to be protected by the male members of the society. Because of this reason females cannot suggest or protest. This is the first step of subjugation and suppression. According to her; even the educated females have the double identity – professional and private.

Another finding of her research was that the income of the women is not considered as the main financial source for the family, but as supplementary to the income of their males. She also found that those results were not valid for the upper and advanced families, where complete freedom is given to their females.

Vijaya Mani (2013) has uncovered the central point impacting the Work Life Parity of Ladies experts in India, for example, part clash, absence of acknowledgment, authoritative governmental issues, sex separation, elderly and youngsters consideration issues, nature of wellbeing, issues in time administration and absence of fitting social backing.

RESEARCH METHODOLOGY:

1. This research is based on both primary and secondary data.
2. The author surveyed males and females of different age groups by mailing them questionnaire.
3. Data was also collected from various websites to back up the data collected through survey.
4. A total of 80 mails were sent in which 58 responses were received.
5. The results are based on data collected from-

38% males and 62% females i.e.

36 females

22 males

Age group varying from 15-55 with divisions

15-25: 12

25-35: 10

35-45: 16

45-55: 20

Professions being
12 students
24 employed
8 unemployed
14 business owners

DATA ANALYSIS (from the survey collected)
Graph 1 :
20.7% voted "no" in which 19% were women.
70% were students and unemployed people also voted no.
10% people weren't sure about it and thus voted for "maybe", in which 45% were men and 55% women.

OBSERVATION-

People are uncertain about the working conditions or facilities of female employees because there are not enough or no female employees in their working firm in urban areas. High percentage of females (employed-unemployed) voted no. Maximum proportion of students and unemployed people voted no based on either their observations from surroundings, previous experience or even theoretical knowledge.

CAUSE-

Gender divide- There still exists biasness and discrimination between males and females' employees. Women aren't always given equal wages, opportunities and chances as are their male counterparts due to various reasons one of them being conservative mindset of society.

Less wages: Despite gains in some areas, women earn an average of just two-thirds of men's wages. Wage discrimination is decreasing in the developed world, albeit slowly. And in some countries, there has been little or no change. This pay gap is wide in India with women in the country earning 19% less than men, according to monster salary index (MSI).

Graph 2:

40% people voted for "not always" in which 32% were women.

42% people who voted for 'no' and 'not always' were employed or in business.

OBSERVATION-

People still feel that promotions aren't always based on individual performance, most of them are women. Even males in business feel women aren't given equal chances.

CAUSE- biasness and discrimination still persistent in businesses and working firms.

Graph 3 :

Almost 28% people voted for "can't say" in which 62% were women and 38% men.

60% of people who voted for 'no' or 'can't say' belonged to working population.

OBSERVATION-

People are uncertain about facilities because there barely

are that many. Due to limited number of female employees, companies do not develop all working facilities and suitable working conditions for women. These limitations hamper the recruitment of women and eventually the growth of women and economy.

CAUSE- Unsuitable and limited facilities like-

Maternity coverage: Despite the measures taken, nearly 60% of women do not have a statutory right to maternity leave, and almost 66% are not legally entitled to paid maternity leave. This lack of coverage has a major impact on women's ability to hold down steady jobs and can stop them from returning to work after childbirth.

Lack of transport and social protection: In developing and emerging countries, the lack of safe and accessible transportation and social protection is the most challenging factor for women who report being affected by this. All too often, women risk facing harassment and even sexual assault on their daily commute and higher incidences of informal work.

Graph 4 :

OBSERVATION-

Young women aged 20-30 still feel there are scarcity of opportunities. Unconscious bias still exists and women are restricted when it comes to certain jobs. Most of the unemployed people mostly belonging to the age group 40-

50 felt women don't have wide range of options or opportunities which seems to be generated from their personal experience.

CAUSE-

Gender divide and Scarcity of opportunities: women feel that they aren't always provided with the best opportunities and promotions as are their male counterparts. They're also restricted from certain jobs especially related to labour or government. LinkedIn Opportunity Index 2021 that as many as 85 per cent women in India have missed out on a raise, promotion or other work offers because of their gender.

OTHER OBSERVATIONS MADE-

OBSERVATION- Middle aged women of 40-50 years prefer looking after their homes. Socio-cultural norms and family non- allowance hold women back.

CAUSE - Socio- cultural norms like-

Gender roles and pressure to conform: Across India, there are cultural expectations that married women should not work and prioritise housework and care work. A survey on social attitudes in 2016 found that around 40-60% of men and women believe married women should not work if the husband earns reasonably well.

Work-family balance: Work such as childcare and maintenance are necessary for a household's welfare – and therefore for the well-being of societies as a whole – but women still shoulder the brunt of this often invisible and undervalued workload. Men consider themselves free from household responsibilities. Globally, the lack of affordable care for children or family members is also an obstacle only for women in work.

Unpaid work: People generally try to find the answer to the question why women work less than men whereas in reality when both paid and unpaid work are taken in account, women frequently work longer hours than men. On average, women spend nearly three times more hours on unpaid household and care work than men.

BRIDGING THE GAP:

ASSERTING INDEPENDENTNESS: women should be encouraged to be financially and socially independent. This will promote equality in true sense and instill confidence in women eventually increasing working rates.

ACHIEVE EQUAL PAY: women's rights of equal value and pay should be protected by law and promoted in practice. Gender neutral job and work transparency can help overcome this divide. Strengthening existing systems such as minimum wages and collective bargaining might also help.

PROVISION OF EDUCATION AND SKILLS: women should be educated and more importantly, educated women should be encouraged to build a career and work rather than being bound to home chores. Government should fund entrepreneurship courses or ones which provide skills.

ELIMINATE DISCRIMINATION: men and women's work should be evaluated equally with equal ratio of pay, promotions and facilities. Women should speak against discrimination faced and should be provided with job security.

PROMOTE FAMILY-WORK BALANCE: men should equally take the responsibility of household chores, giving same amount of time at work and at home as they expect their spouses to do. For that, they should be educated and encouraged to change society's mindset and promote working.

CREATE QUALITY CARE JOBS: policies providing suitable and safe working conditions and facilities should be promoted and implemented. Women should receive maternity coverage, social protection and suitable working conditions.

CONCLUSION:

Despite of the developments made, women still lag behind and faces obstacles in working on many levels. They want to be in paid employment, but a persistent set of socio-economic barriers keep them out of the workforce. Identifying and quantifying these barriers allows us to develop smarter policies for eliminating them. Ultimately closing gender gaps in the labour force is not just good for women and their household, but for national and global economy as well.

Dynamics of Migration and Development

Mr. Raghav M Garg
Author Bio : Mr. Raghav M Garg is a Student, 16 years old studying in G.D. Goenka school, passionate about debating and research. Field of interest is politics and economics and likes to read about it.

Dynamics of Migration and Development

INTRODUCTION :

During the covid times, India observed the problem faced by migrant workers. Thousands of landless labourers had started walking towards their home states due to unemployment. The study focuses on relation between migration and development in detail.

STATEMENT OF PROBLEM:

"To identify relation between development and migration"

OBJECTIVES :

- Determining problems faced by people due to migration.
- Determining the changes required to adapt after

migration.
- Determining if migration acts as an opportunity with special emphasis on economic sectors.

REASEARCH METHDOLOGY:

- The study material is based on survey collected from group of people via google forms.
- Data is analysed on the basis of responses and solutions collected as well as statistics from trusted sources.

Analysis of data :

Graph 1 :

LITERAL REVIEW :

Over 60 percent of the people think that they suffer problems due to migration whereas 24 percent people have problems partly.
Further, analysing the major problems caused to due to migration.

Graph 2:

HYPOTHESIS PROBLEM 1 (different culture):

On the basis of responses collected 29.4 percent people believe that different culture is the major problem caused due to migration. Different culture and ethnicity stand a major role in migration. People migrating from oppressed minorities might face tensions in forming a new habitual environment.

HYPOTHESIS PROBLEM 2 (different language):

According to UNESCO more than 50 percent population is multi linguistic, but migrant workers especially from under developed country face lot of issues in communicating in developed countries. A women migrated from Ukraine to USA faced difficulties communicating in English, she had misinterpreted the contract given to her which further led to exploitation.

HYPOTHESIS PROBLEM 3 (different lifestyle):

Migration brings the opportunity of communication between various communities as seen in the Janardhan Case where small ethnic groups develop with co relation of big ethnic groups. But various group of society face the most difficulties here, among the responses collected maximum percentage of people believe that lifestyle adapting and change is biggest problem.

Graph 3:

LITERAL REVIEW :

Detailed analysis of the sectors represent the preference of migrants to travel and view opportunities.

Hypothesis 4 – Considering industrial sector to be the maximum ;

As per census 2011 in INDIA, 13 percent migrants are from different state , travelling from rural sector to urban as a result for dense population in various states for INDIA. In recent pandemic industrial labour were the ones most affected. In search of workforce migrant workers are given jobs in industrial sector. Often exploitation can be observed in various parts of country.

Hypothesis 5 – Analysing the reasons for less response among migration:

As per recent reports published over 90 percent of the Indian farmers use their own fields to cultivate crops, the amount of capital investment to the rate of employment is very low. The case of small villages is quite evident of the fact that modern reforms have not reached various parts of the country and our not accepted. Thus lacks potential investors in the field.

Conclusion :

It was an attempt made to put light on various aspects related to migration and migrants. Various social reasons have been briefly incorporated under the information provided and hypothesis put forward. The facts and figures have been taken from references and the analysis relies on the author as well as responses collected.

Income Inequality, Poverty and Economic Welfare

Ms. UditiGupta
Author Bio: Ms. UditiGupta is a Student researcher at 15, extremely intrigued by economic welfare and the connected field. Fondness towards research about the condition of people in various sectors.

Income Inequality, Poverty and Economic Welfare

Abstract :

Rounds of the National Sample Survey. The behaviour of important microeconomic aggregates is used to explain observed changes in inequality and poverty. The post-reform period has been marked by a substantial growth in rural and, particularly, urban inequality, as well as a small decrease in poverty.

The rise in inequality can be explained by an increase in the relative proportion of output going to capital v/s labour, a decrease in the rate of labour absorption, and the rapid expansion of the services sector. Higher growth's poverty reducing impacts have been harmed by rising inequality.

Regional inequality has also widened as a result of the reforms. This is especially true in the case of rural poverty, although it also applies to urban poor to a lesser level. In terms of inequality, poverty, and real mean consumption, statistical convergence between states is modest. Several policy recommendations are made.

INTRODUCTION :

The objective of economic expansion must be to improve the poor's living conditions. Economic growth that does not result in significant and long-term reductions in poverty may exacerbate rather than cure problems. Similarly, if rapid expansion is achieved at the expense of a worsening in resource distribution, it will eventually become unsustainable, since social tensions would arise. Indeed, it is plausible to envision a situation in which economic expansion exacerbates inequality to the point where poverty raises.

The conventional belief in India is that the trend rate of economic growth was low and stable for a long time. A breach was made by the liberalisation of trade and investment, as well as economic changes, which began in 1991. As a result, the trend rate of economic growth increased dramatically. The question that emerges here is: How has India's economic growth affected inequality and poverty levels? The goal of this research is to come up with some preliminary conclusions on this crucial topic.

India has opted for slow and controlled liberalisation, downplaying the importance of the Washington consensus' emphasis on reform pace. There are also variances in the details. As a result, with the exception of IMF monies obtained in 1991, reliance on foreign bilateral or multilateral public capital inflows 3 has been limited. As a result of the reforms, policymakers are dealing with a tight government budget restriction rather than a potentially dangerous foreign payments position. The Delhi consensus stressed gradual trade liberalisation and privatisation while avoiding capital account reform.

This cautious approach has avoided big shocks, and the increases in inequality that have resulted from these reforms have been minor by comparison to, say, transition economies. Rural inequality has risen at a slower rate than urban inequality, and total inequality has risen at a faster rate.

LITERATURE REVIEW :

Income Inequality in India

In economics, income inequality refers to a large gap in income distribution between people, groups, communities, social classes, or countries. Inequality in income is a fundamental aspect of social stratification and class. Many other types of inequality, such as money, political power, and social status disparities, impact and are affected by it. Income is a fundamental predictor of quality of life, affecting the health and wellbeing of individuals and families, and it varies according to social factors such as sex, age, race, and ethnicity.

On a worldwide scale, income inequality is high by any standard, with the richest 1% of the world's population receiving as much as the poorest 56% in the early twenty-first century. Income disparity in the United States is substantially higher than in most other industrialised countries. In 2014, the richest 1% of Americans collected 22% of total income, while the top 10% of American households received roughly 60% of total income.

India's Gini coefficient, which is a measure of income distribution inequality, was 35.2 in 2011, according to the CIA World Fact book, ranking 95th out of 157 countries. As of November 2016, one survey estimated that 54 percent of the country's wealth is controlled by millionaires, the second most behind Russia. The richest one percent of Indians holds 58 percent of the country's wealth, while the richest ten percent own 80 percent. This pattern has continued, implying that the wealthy are becoming wealthier at a quicker rate than the poor, expanding the income disparity. Since the institution of income tax in 1922, inequality has risen, surpassing the British Raj's record of 20.7 percent of national income held by the top 1% in 1939–40.

Because of huge gaps in income tax data, it is impossible to effectively evaluate wealth disparity in India, according to Thomas Piketty. Between 1997 and 2000, official data showed several discrepancies, whereas between 2000 and

2012, no data was provided. Then, in 2013, official income tax data revealed that just 1% of Indians paid taxes that year, with only 2% filing a tax return.
Because of the scarcity of accurate data, it is nearly hard to draw meaningful, quantifiable conclusions concerning income disparity in India.

India's economy continues to expand, with its GDP increasing at a quicker rate than most other countries. However, an increase in the country's GDP does not imply greater income equality. In India, rising income disparity has hampered impoverished people's access to education and healthcare. As income disparity rises, it becomes more difficult for the poor to rise up the economic ladder, increasing their likelihood of falling into poverty. Low pay, long working hours, and a lack of essential amenities like as first aid, drinking water, and sanitation define the poorest 10% of the population.

Poverty in India :

Poverty is defined when a segment of society is unable to meet even the most basic needs. The Indian Planning Commission established a poverty criterion based on suggested daily dietary needs of 2,400 calories for rural regions and 2,100 calories for urban areas. The average calorie need is calculated using the population composition by age, gender, and profession categories, as well as the Indian Council of Medical Research's calorie guidelines.

The poverty line in rupees is the midpoint of the spending

class when calorie needs are met. On this basis, the rural and urban cut-off points for 1991-92 prices are Rs. 181.50 and Rs. 209.60, respectively. The poverty line has been set at Rs. 10,890 for a family of five in rural regions and Rs. 12,570 in urban areas for a family of five.

For the last few years, the method of identifying those living in poverty in India has been mired in dispute. The National Sample Study Organization's survey was used by the Planning Commission to define the poverty line and determine the number of people living below it. Based on these criteria, the Planning Commission determined that 18.96 percent of the entire population was poor in 1993-94. The percentage of individuals living in poverty has decreased significantly over the previous two decades, from 51.3 percent in 1977-78 to 26.1 percent in 1999-2000. The aim for the Tenth Five-Year Plan (2002-07) is to reduce poverty by 5 percentage points to 19.3 percent by 2007. In 2007, the poverty objectives for rural and urban areas are 21.1 percent and 15.1 percent, respectively.

Economic Welfare in India :

The distribution of commodities and resources to promote social wellbeing is referred to as welfare. It is concerned with the allocation of resources in an economically efficient manner for the benefit of the people. Welfare seeks to steer public policy in such a way that distribution benefits all members of society economically and socially. The goal of welfare economics is to improve society's overall wellbeing. As a result, welfare economics entails assessing economic strategies and influencing public policy for the better good of society. The methods of cost-benefit analysis and social welfare functions are used in the study of welfare economics.

There are several factors for determining whether the benefits of a change in the economy would outweigh any disadvantages. When looking at Pareto efficiency, it's impossible to distribute resources to make one person better off without making one or more people worse off. The cost-benefit analysis is based on the idea that utility gains and losses can be quantified in terms of money. Welfare economics aims to attain a situation in which a society's overall pleasure is maximised while also maximising producer and consumer surplus in the many markets that make up the society.

METHODOLOGY :

Through this study, the question of why one needs to know about Income inequality, poverty and economic welfare is dealt with. Further, this study talks about the objective of economic expansion, that is, to improve the poor's living conditions. In addition, this study states the current scenario about Income inequality, poverty and economic welfare in India as well as in the global world. It also gives information about the past steps, reforms, policies made for the poor by various surveys.

This study is highly based on Qualitative approach as it clears the idea of poverty, poverty studies separate three dimensions: economic wellbeing, social exclusion, and capacity. Economic wellbeing is determined by whether or not a person has enough money to obtain a baseline level of consumption or human welfare. Second, poverty might be seen as a result of the poor's social isolation from the rest of society. Finally, poverty is a result of a lack of individual capabilities, such as education or health care, those are required to achieve a basic degree of human wellbeing.

The data gathering methods used to identify the impoverished in India are as follows. The poverty level was based on a Uniform Resource Period (URP) from 1993 to 1994, which involves interviewing people about their consumption spending over a 30-day period. From 2000 onwards, the NSSO used a Mixed Reference Period (MRP) approach to estimate consumption of five low frequency items over a 30-day period. Clothing, durable goods, education, and institutional health expenditures are among them.

CONCLUSION :

Poverty estimation is necessary:

To Assess the Impact of Welfare Programs: Estimating poverty is crucial because it allows us to assess the impact and success of various government programs designed to alleviate poverty. Furthermore, these methods may be adjusted to remedy any flaws that may exist. It's part of a Poverty Elimination Plan: Poverty estimations are used to create new strategies to guarantee that poverty is eradicated

from society.
It's a Constitutional Requirement: The Indian Constitution guarantees a just and equitable society, and poverty assessment facilitates this by making identifying the vulnerable portions of society simple.

Little is known about how doctors describe poverty, their attitudes toward disadvantaged patients, or their perceptions of those patients' attitudes toward health and the healthcare system. The purpose of this study is to investigate these beliefs and attitudes in order to gain a better understanding of how GPs approach the problem of poverty and their recommendations for improving healthcare for the poor.

To sum up everything that has been stated so far, several programmes (e.g., IRDP, JRY) have been implemented by the Indian government and state governments to eradicate poverty in India. While the goals of these programmes are admirable, they are predicated on the erroneous assumption that spending money is a necessary and sufficient prerequisite for poverty reduction. This attitude downplays the importance of non-monetary policies and their influence on people's lives. Many grassroots workers have observed that some government policies often affect the poor far more than the benefits they receive from money-oriented programmes like the IRDP.

SUGGESTIONS :

Nelson Mandela said, "As long as poverty, inequality and

gross inequality persist in our world, none of us can truly rest." As we can see that equality among the rich and poor plays a crucial role in a country, here are some suggestions to provide income equality, and reduce the gap btw the rich and the poor: Develop and execute policies and initiatives in areas such as health, education, nutrition, and sanitation that will allow the poor to participate in and contribute to economic progress. According to studies, a ten percent rise in a country's average income decreases poverty by 20-30%.

Water and other natural resources should be better managed. The majority of the rural poor rely on agriculture or other natural resources to survive. As a result, more fair access to such resources is required in order for them to properly manage their resources.
Invest in agricultural programmes and put them in place. Since 1978, China has assisted 800 million individuals in escaping poverty. The Agricultural Bank of China will finance more than $400 billion to assist develop rural regions, fund education, infrastructure, and food production as part of its aim to eradicate poverty by 2020.

Encourage countries to use trade as a means of escaping poverty. Growth and prosperity are dependent on trade. Indonesia, Botswana, and Brazil, among the world's poorest countries, have traded their way out of poverty.

Create and increase work and income opportunities, as well as cultivate entrepreneurial skills.
Providing fundamental social services such as education, health care, appropriate food, sanitation, housing, and

clean water to all people. Developing progressive social protection measures to assist individuals who are unable to sustain themselves. Empower individuals who are poor by including them in the formulation and execution of poverty-reduction and-eradication policies and activities.

REFERENCES ;

1. "Country Comparison - Gini Index".cia.gov. Central Intelligence Agency. Retrieved 3 February 2020.
2. ^ Jump up to: ab"India second most 'unequal' country after Russia: Report".dailypioneer.com. 4 September 2016. Retrieved 1 March 2019.
3. ^From British Raj to Billionaire Raj, Economic and Political Weekly, 7 October 2017
4. https://www.downtoearth.org.in/news/economy/how-india-remains-poor-it-willtake-7-generations-for-india-s-poor-to-reach-mean-income--68898
5. ^ Jump up to: ab Martin Ravallion, Shaohua Chen and Prem Sangraula (2008). "Dollar a Day Revisited"(PDF). The World Bank.
6. ^ Jump up to: abc"Country Briefing: India, Multidimensional Poverty Index (MPI) At a Glance"(PDF). Oxford Poverty and Human Development Initiative. Retrieved 16 August 2017.
7. UNESCO (2019).Global education monitoring report 2019: gender report: Buildingbridges for gender equality. UNESCO.ISBN978-92-3-100329-5.Archivedfrom the original on 6 December 2019. Retrieved 5 March 2020.
8. ^Jump up to:abcdDugger, Celia W. (5 December 2009)."Aid gives alternatives toAfrican orphanages". The

New York Times.Archivedfrom the original on 26 May 2017. Retrieved 18 February 2017.

The Invisible Hand Supply & Demand of the Covid 19 Vaccine

Ms. Mehak Gupta

Author Bio: Ms. Mehak Gupta is a Student, Researcher and reader of 15, greatly interested in learning about social issues. Mehak is a trained Bharatnatyam dancer who believes that art is the greatest influencer. She hopes to one day to create economic policies to benefit the underprivileged.

The Invisible Hand: Supply & Demand of the Covid 19 Vaccine

ABSTRACT:

The covid 19 pandemic coupled with lockdown affected all sections of the economy. The halt in good production and its subsidiary activities created a unique situation that required to be studied. The covid 19 vaccine however was an anomaly unto itself . It was an almost perfectly inelastic good with minimal fixed price. The demand and supply of the vaccine in the market was affected by various factors such as its availability and its effectiveness. The article elaborates on the concept of Supply and Demand and then analyses the vaccine through that lens.

TERMINOLOGY;

Demand, Supply, Law Of Marginal Utility, Law Of Demand, Law Of Supply, Price, Quantity Demanded, Quantity Supplied, Equilibrium, Commodities, Vaccine , Daily Vaccination Rate, Vaccine procurement

INTRODUCTION:

The following section describes demand and supply in the simplest of forms. These definitions assume perfect competition in market, free entry and exit in market, rational consumers also factor other than price which affect sales are constant. These factors include

- Changes in taste
- Changes in the economy
- Income of consumers
- Long term changes in production

DEMAND:

Demand is defined as the rate at which consumers want to buy a product. According to Economics Theory it consists of 2 main factors.

1. Willingness

This is the desire for the good and it determines the disposition to buy the good at a specific price.

2. Ability

This is the possession of sufficient income or wealth to buy the good at a specific price.

However, both factors of demand depend on the market price. When the market price for a product is high, the demand will be low. When price is low, demand is high.

At very low prices, many consumers will be able to purchase a product. But people usually want only so much of a good. As per the Law of Diminishing Marginal Utility acquiring additional increments of a good or service in some time period will yield less and less satisfaction. Therefore, the demand for a product at low prices is limited by taste and is not infinite even when the price equals zero. As the price increases, the same amount of money will purchase fewer products. When the price for a product is very high, the demand will decrease because, while consumers may wish to purchase a product very much, they are limited by their ability to buy.

DEMAND CURVE

The given figure generalizes the relationship between price of a good and the quantity a consumer is willing to buy at a given point of time. It's called a Simple Demand Curve.

The figure implies that price of a commodity is the only factor that affects its demand. However, that is not the case in actuality, other influencing factors are assumed to be constant.

LAW OF DEMAND:

Economics is the study of usage of limited means to satisfy unlimited wants. The Law of Demand focuses on these unlimited wants.

The Law of Demand holds that quantity purchased varies inversely with price of the commodity. That is, consumers use the first units of an economic good they purchase to serve their most urgent needs first, and use each additional unit of the good to serve successively lower-valued ends. Naturally, people prioritize more urgent wants and needs over less urgent ones in their economic behaviour, and this carries over into how people choose among the limited means available to them. For any economic good, the first unit of that good that a consumer gets their hands on will tend to be put to use to satisfy the most urgent need the consumer has that that good can satisfy.

SUPPLY:

Supply is defined as the quantity of goods a firm offers to sell in the market at a given price. Willingness and the ability to supply determine the seller's actions. The higher the prices , the more the quantity of commodity will be available to the consumers. This is due to the fact that suppliers are able to maintain an over all profit despite the higher costs of production that result from expansion of their capacity.

Each specific good or service has its own supply and demand patterns based on price, utility and personal preference. If people demand a good and are willing to pay more for it, producers will add to the supply. As the supply increases, the price will fall given the same level of demand. In a market, when the inventory is less than the desired inventory, manufacturers raise both the supply of their product and its price. The short-term increase in supply makes manufacturing costs rise, causing increase in price. The price change in turn increases the desired rate of production. A similar effect occurs if inventory is too high.

Ideally, markets will reach a point ofequilibrium where the supply equals the demand (no excess supply and no shortages) for a given price point; at this point, consumer utility and producer profits are maximized.

There are 5 types of supply.

1. Market
2. Short term
3. Long term
4. Joint
5. Composite

SUPPLY CURVE

It's a graphical representation of the correlation between the cost of the commodity and the quantity supplied for the given period of time.

The given supply curve tends to curve upwards because each additional unit of the commodity created is assumed to be more difficult or expensive than its predecessor. Therefore, each successive unit requires a higher price to justify its cost of production.

There are 2 types of supply curves.

1. Individual

2. Market

LAW OF SUPPLY:

The law of supply holds that the price of commodity and the quantity offered by suppliers are proportional in nature, given that all other influencing factors are constant. suppliers can choose how much of their goods to produce and later bring to market. At any given point of time the supply that sellers bring to market is fixed, and sellers simply face a decision to either sell or withhold their stock from a sale; consumer demand sets the price and sellers can only charge what the market will bear. If consumer demand rises over time, the price will rise, and suppliers can choose devoted new resources to production (or new suppliers can enter the market) which increases the quantity supplied. Demand ultimately sets the price in a competitive market, supplier response to the price they can expect to receive sets the quantity supplied.
INTERACTION BETWEEN DEMAND AND SUPPLY:

Demand is the quantity of a commodity consumers are willing and able to purchase. Supply is the quantity of a commodity at each given price available for purchase. Supply and demand interact with each other to control the market.

Buyers and sellers react inversely to change in price of a commodity. With the increase in price the willingness and ability of consumers to buy a commodity decreases. This relationship leads to a downward sloping demand curve.

However, with increase in prise the willingness and ability of suppliers to sell the commodity increases. This results in an upward sloping supply curve. The point where the two curves intersect is the point of equilibrium

EFFECT OF COVID 19 ON SUPPLY AND DEMAND:

According to psychologist Robert Cialdini " a product becomes more attractive when their perceived availability is limited" . this creates a psychological need for the product in a consumer's mind. During the covid 19 outbreak this was apparent. Low supply of commodities created a higher demand and the price of commodities increased.

During the lockdown demand for essential items demand for essential items was through the roofs. Milk, lentils, flour, sugar et cetra had a lower supply than what the demand was. Consumers were in a state of uncertainty and therefore desired to be prepared for any scenario. So as the supply of products decreased due to halted production businesses were able to make greater profits by increasing prices.

However inessential business owners were not so fortunate. From the consumer perspective , non-essential items were now viewed as unattainable or considered a luxury of a high value due to limited income .therefore following the Law of Demand consumers stopped investing in non-essential commodities.

Therefore, in conjunction of with not knowing the extent of the lockdown , the principle shifted and both supply and demand changed. Although a certain number of businesses were not majorly affected other businesses were unable to make a profit, with many unable to stay afloat, causing a significant number of businesses to fall into administration or permanent closure.

COVID 19 VACCINELAUNCHING THE CAMPAIGN ;

The press information bureau made the details of India's Covid Vaccination Strategy public on the 19th of April 2021. Created by the National Expert Group on Vaccine Administration for COVID-19 it focused on the scale and speed for the third phase.

The first phase of India's COVID-19 mass inoculation programme was launched on 16 January, covering an estimated 30 million healthcare and front-line workers. On the first of March, the country initiated the second phase, aiming to cover people above-45 with co-morbidities and the cohort above 60. This was expanded on 1 April to cover everyone above 45 years, bringing the total to over 300 million people, accounting for the high-risk and most vulnerable, accounting for 80 percent of recorded Covid mortality in the country.

In April the country suffered the massive onslaught of the second wave of infection. At the peak of the first wave in 2020 in mid-September, India registered 96,000 new cases of infection daily; by 18 April, the daily cases had surpassed 275,000, reaching an all-time high of over 400,000 cases in early May. Daily deaths recorded a steep curve too, crossing 4,500 briefly, and has remained high since.

Due to the sudden increase in deaths the third phase of the vaccination strategy was begun on 1st May. The phase included all those above the age of 18 therefore adding 600 million candidates for the vaccine. Although the vaccine for people between the age of 18-45 could either be free or priced according to the state governments.

Approved vaccine producers—Serum Institute of India (SII), producing Covishield; and Bharat Biotech (BB), producing Covaxin—would supply 50 percent of their monthly production from 1 May onwards to the central government. The balance was earmarked for state governments and private hospitals. Both aspects of the decision—opening up to the 18-45 cohort, and dual pricing—were justified as introducing decentralisation and flexibility.

DEMAND SUPPLY MISMATCH:

As the death rate due to covid cases increased and vaccination opened up the consumers led to chaos. The initial lukewarm response to the vaccine roll out was replaced by large crowds flocking the vaccination centres and returning without the shot. The vaccine shortages were blamed on wither the central and state government or on the producers. Some states had to even halt vaccination drives for 18- to 45-year-olds due to lack of supplies.

Analysts tried to explain and provide reasons behind the shortages but the task was difficult due to lack of information. However, the new disclosure of the below given procurement approach has provided some answers.

From the total production the Centre has been restricted to 50 % of the procurements since May . Given that 110 million doses of Covishield and 50 million doses of Covaxin were purchased directly by the state governments and private hospitals between July and may. The stats bring total availability till July end to –

Organisation
No Of Doses (In Millions)

Central Govt

356

State Govt

100

Private Hospitals

60

Total

516

However, given the production capacity of BB it's unlikely that it would have 50 million doses to spare after fulfilling its commitments to the Centre. This mis match between demand and supply explained the drop-in daily vaccination rate from 3.6 to 1.56 million in may despite the strategy now covering a wider rage to consumers due to the 18 to 45 age range.

If the production schedules were able to keep pace, the balance 316 million doses were delivered and exports were halted the daily vaccination rate could be increased to 5 million doses . however, given India s situation with ever climbing death rates and quicker rollout of vaccines being an urgent requirement the targets are too modest, even to prepare for the looming 3rd wave.

A quick vaccine rollout is the country's only way through. In a clear sign of acceleration, the government of India informed the public on 30 May that while a little more than 79 million doses of COVID-19 vaccine were available with the states in May, nearly 120 million doses will be made available in June. The May-June combined availability of 200 million doses also suggests that any raw material shortages may have been significantly resolved.

To address the future mis-match , it's necessary to monitor the supply side .

The SII had an initial capacity of about 50 million doses a month, along with a stockpile of 50 million doses in January, it currently averages 65 million doses a month. BB too had a monthly production of over 5 million doses in January, along with a stockpile of 20 million. Once the

Bangalore facility came online, the production shot up, and is now at 20 million doses. In addition to these 66 million doses were exported as well .

In the third week of April the Centre began providing financial aid to production companies to increase production. Advances of INR 30,000 million and INR 15,000 million respectively, were announced for the two companies. In addition, three public sector undertakings—Haffkine Institute, Bharat Biologicals and Immunological (BIBCOL), and Indian Immunological (IIL)—have been provided INR 1,550 million by the Centre to upgrade facilities and undertake production of at least 30 million Covaxin doses per month.
On may 9 an affidavit indicating the aim to produce 65 and 20 million doses by SII and BB respectively was filed by the centre with the Supreme Court. The following week, SII and BB also filed monthly production plans for the period of June September with the Drug Controller General of India. However, these monthly supply figures currently do not support a target of 10 million daily vaccinations.

NEXT STEPS:

An effective response to the pandemic requires a tree fold approach.

1. Treatment of the affected
2. Slowing the spread of virus
3. Protection of the unexposed.

The following strategies are suggested to systematically control the virus.

• Strategic monthly planning.
Both Centre and states must initiate specific monthly schedules for vaccination. This will help in monitoring the progress of vaccination across geographies and evaluating bottlenecks in the vaccine delivery process in a timely manner. Such a system will also make governments responsible for the proper and timely resolution of issues. Complete transparency must be introduced in the allocation to states to ensure greater trust and coordination.

• Targeted vaccination campaigns and Risk communication. Given the vaccine shortages that have been reported across the country, the high-risk populations as well as potential super-spreader groups among the active and mobile populations need to be actively identified and inoculated in an intensified campaign mode. Local governments, health workers, and community, political as well as religious leaders will have to be incentivised to help identify and vaccinate the most vulnerable. India should remain vigilant in the enforcement of appropriate social distancing behaviours, preventing large gatherings, increasing testing levels, and tracking the spread of the virus by targeted genome sequencing and sharing of data.

• Proactive procurement and expanding manufacturing capacity. Government agencies must start engaging constructively with vaccine developers and producers to anticipate raw material requirements and ensure maintenance of necessary supply lines. This also means fast tracking development and regulatory approvals with regard to the vaccines currently in different stages of development and trials.

REFRENCES:

https://www.investopedia.com/articles/economics/11/intro-supplydemand.asp

https://ocw.mit.edu/courses/sloan-school-of-management/15-988system-dynamics-self-study-fall-1998-spring-1999/readings/economics.pdf

Press Information Bureau, 'Government of India announces aliberalised and Accelerated Phase 3 Strategy of Covid-19 Vaccinationfrom 1st May', April 19 2021.

Press Information Bureau,Press briefing on the actions taken, preparedness and updates on COVID-19, Dated: 13.05.2021, May 13 2021.

Ministry of Health and Family Welfare, Government of India,Covid-19 Vaccine Operational Guidelines, December 28 2020.

Payal Banerjee, 'Central govt asks Serum, Bharat Biotech to cut vaccineprices', The Indian Express, April 27, 2021.

Kriti Kapur, 'Availability of vaccine supplies in India', Observer Research Foundation.

'Going global for the jabs: Tenders out, responses not in', The Indian Express, 24 May 2021.

Pricilla Jebaraj,Vaccines bought first using PM CARES funds cost Centremore,The Hindu, 7 May 2021.

Oommen C Kurian, 'Next three months of the world's

largestvaccination drive: Managing expectations', Observer Research Foundation, 4 May 2021.

Ministry of Health and Family Welfare,COVID-19 Vaccination as on: 21May 2021, 08:00 IST.

[10]'More Than 1.81 Billion Shots Given: Covid-19 Tracker', Bloomberg Vaccine tracker, May 21, 2021.

Government of India, "Update on COVID Vaccine Allocation", Press Information Bureau, May 30, 2021.

Seema Singh and MaitriPorecha, 'Covid Taskforce, let's get real on vaccines. It's time for plan B', The Ken, May 27, 2021,https://theken.com/story/covid-taskforce-lets-get-real-on-vaccines-its-time-forplan-b/

Ministry of External Affairs, Covid-19 Vaccine Maitri: Vaccine Supply, assessed at 1000 hours on May 20 2021,https://www.mea.gov.in/vaccine-supply.htm

'Centre approves Rs 3000 cr funds for Serum Institute, Rs 1500 cr forBharat Biotech to ramp up vaccine production', India Today, April 19 2021.

'India readies state-run firms to manufacture Covaxin', Live Mint, May 16 2021,https://www.livemint.com/news/india/india-readies-staterun-firms-to-manufacture-covaxin-11621078961652.html

'India readies state-run firms to manufacture Covaxin', Live Mint, May 16 2021,https://www.livemint.com/news/india/india-readies-staterun-firms-to-manufacture-covaxin-11621078961652.html

'AFFIDAVIT DATED 09.05.2021, ON BEHALF OF THE UNION OF INDIA', Live Law,https://www.livelaw.in/pdf_upload/centres-affidavitin-suo-moto-covid-case-supreme-court-

393164.pdf
Oommen C Kurian, 'Vaccination a globally integrated enterprise: CLsare not a quick-fix solution', Hindustan Times, 24 May 2021.
[19]'India readies state-run firms to manufacture Covaxin', Live Mint, May 16 2021.
Oommen C Kurian, 'Next three months of the world's largest vaccination drive: Managing expectations', Observer Research Foundation, 4 May 2021, https://www.orfonline.org/expertspeak/next-three-months-of-the-worlds-largest-vaccination-drive/

Resource Geopolitics and International Relations

Ms.Anya Jain

Author Bio: Ms. Anya Jain is a Student Researcher at 15, extremely intrigued by financial matters and the connected field. Exceptionally quick to find out with regards to the foreign relations, economies and world front and center concerns.

Resource Geopolitics and International Relations

ABSTRACT :

Resource Geopolitics is all about who gets what, when, where, and how in resource geopolitics.

Global power shifts in the post Cold-War era have characteristically moved away from traditional military rivalries to economic expansion and prowess. The paradigm, in part fuelled by technological advances and the ferocious scale of globalization in recent decades, has highlighted the strategic advantages lent in particular by natural resources. Historically linked to prolonged conflicts and civil wars in parts of Africa, Latin America and Asia, natural resources such as hydrocarbons, gold, uranium, diamonds, copper, zinc and rare earth minerals are now increasingly reshaping the global geopolitical landscape, influencing foreign policies and boosting economic growth engines across continents. Rapid industrialization, rising demand for energy, emergence of new markets and depletion of natural resources at a disconcerting rate, are all adding to a growing rivalry among nations for access and control of resources and precious minerals.

The enviable oil wealth of the Middle East, which has allowed the region for over 50 years to monopolize global oil supplies, production and prices through its OPEC cartel, is now a classic text-book example of how natural resources can critically mold foreign policies and forge enduring political ties.

IMPORTANCE OF NATURAL RESOURCES ;

The delicate balance between economic interests and global political discourse is becoming increasingly precarious as the demand for raw commodities and resources grows tremendously. The West's cautious attitude to Iran's contentious nuclear programme is driven by security concerns as much as economic concerns. The imminent threat by Tehran to close the Strait of Hormuz, which transports 40% of the world's tanker-borne oil, amid rising pressure to halt its ambitious nuclear programme, has the potential to crash global markets.

Manipulation of resources to protect national, economic, and security interests has undoubtedly given geopolitical strategies a new dimension. During a diplomatic crisis over a disputed island cluster in the East China Sea in 2010, China halted rare material supplies to Japan for two months, virtually crippling its neighbor's burgeoning electronics sector. China controls the market for rare earth minerals, a group of seventeen elements used in hybrid automobiles, flat-screen televisions, cellphones, computer hard discs, wind turbines, and guided missiles, among other critical modern technology, with 97 percent of world supply share.

Russia, which has the world's greatest natural gas reserves, has a similar monopoly over regional energy trade and a sprawling network of pipelines. Russia, Europe's largest energy supplier, has been accused of price manipulation, transit charge rigging, and diplomatic arm twisting in order to maximise political and financial gains.

Although, increased competition for natural resources, especially to meet energy demands, in recent years has allowed for large scale exploration of new reserves and in the process also boosting developing economies in regions like Latin America, Central Asia and Africa, the rivalry is precariously intertwined with global politics and security.

THE PURSUIT OF GLOBAL RESOURCES :

While influence may be important, governments are often looking for strategic positions because of the desire for natural resources. Natural resources are increasingly widely acknowledged as the new powerful key to defining geopolitics. Natural resources serve as a way of securing economic and strategic interests, as well as a means of achieving wealth. Many examples can be found in the histories of oil, gas, and minerals of how the quest to obtain these resources has both enthralled and propelled world politics and superpower competition.

As a result of the massive demand for resources such as energy, raw materials, food, and water, many battles are taking place in various countries. For example, resource experts predict that the twenty-first century would be marked by "water wars," as population growth puts increased strain on fresh water resources. The various uses to which water can be put can frequently be a source of contention, especially in areas where multiple countries share water. Egypt, for example, sees the Grand Ethiopian Renaissance Dam on the Nile as a threat to its national security. Egypt's position is that if Ethiopia goes ahead with the dam building, it will lose a lot of water. Such "hydro-political difficulties" are particularly likely to erupt in areas served by the Nile, Ganges-Brahmaputra, Indus, Tigris-Euphrates, and Colorado rivers, which are used by several populations and states.

In the twenty-first century, energy has also become a major field of geopolitics and a tool for geopolitical competition. Recently, the idea of "energy security" has become more widely employed in defining international energy politics and guaranteeing that energy issues are considered a part of "high politics." As a result of this evolution, the Middle East has been plagued by international conflicts for the majority of its modern history. Due to its exposure to the bulk of the world's politically and economically unstable regions, the oil and gas business is particularly vulnerable to geopolitical risks.

For years, European nations contended for control of the Middle East's natural resources and geostrategic location by colonising its regions. Since then, the region has been engulfed in a series of severe crises in which superpowers and regional powers fight for territorial influence. With so much strain on resources, it's unavoidable that previously unexplored portions of the globe, such as Antarctica, will be brought into the spotlight. Because of the vast resources available, both the Antarctic and the Arctic have recently received a lot of attention. In these regions, scientific missions have discovered precious minerals. Weather conditions, governance due to the confluence of five bordering countries (Russia, Norway, Canada, the United States, and Denmark), and geopolitical competition between NATO and Russia, whose relations have deteriorated in recent years, are all risks that could affect the region's exploitation. Because progress has been made in certain sovereignty concerns, geopolitical activity in the frozen Arctic has been relatively minimal in the past; yet, there are still contested and unclaimed territories under dispute.

-CHINA:

Under its “go global” policy, China has become much more aggressive in pursuing natural resources from all over the world. The enormous political, economic, and cultural shift in China, from a developing agrarian society to a modern, urban one, has led to some remarkable developments for which the country needs energy surety by searching for foreign energy resources. While iron ore and copper have been the hot targets of overseas acquisitions by Chinese firms, the Chinese have also gone after gold, nickel, tin, and coking coal. It is hard to escape the fact that China, both through its enormous purchasing power and the financial muscle that allows it to make substantial investments in mining and energy resources overseas, is assuming a position of world dominance in the commodities markets.

GLOBALIZATION AND THE SEARCH FOR NATURAL RESOURCES ;

Natural resources play a vital role in globalization, as it brings capital, management, and technology to the host country. Many resource-endowed countries in the developing world, therefore, tend to court MNCs to invest in their countries as they depend on resource exploitation to achieve their developmental goals. This inducement has led to a situation where a number of developing countries have been dovetailed into one big export arena where natural resources are being exploited in order to generate revenue for development. The dominant discourse of multilateral institutions concerning poverty alleviation postulates that MNC investments would help pave the way for economic growth and prosperity.

With this mind, global capitalism and private enterprise have become firmly entrenched as central planks of the development strategy in many resource-endowed countries. But how has this trend impacted on the lives of the people? Who benefits from foreign investment and who loses? How far have the concerns of mining communities shaped the operations of MNCs in these countries? Have the MNCs been able to satisfy the expectations of their host communities? Who appropriates and accumulates rent from resources and how is this done?

The above questions are important to reflect critically on especially when one looks at the role of MNCs in the extractive industry, especially those operating in developing countries. Although many of these countries are aware of the benefits of closer integration of global production and markets, the expected benefits of this phenomenon have largely remained trifling for some of them. By fostering economic growth and the convergence of development styles between developing and developed countries, globalization, in a way has bred tensions on natural resources. Indeed, wider economic and political policies have robbed many developing countries of the chance to become equivalent participants in world affairs. It seems for some of these countries, opportunities for self-enrichment have been inhibited by the inordinate dependence on primary commodities. Undoubtedly, the extreme pressure on natural resources as a basis for economic development has also led to severe environmental problems and human tragedies in many countries.

WHY RENEWABLES WILL TRANSFORM GEOPOLITICS :

The main story of the energy transition is the rise of renewable, particularly solar and wind, and the future decline of fossil fuels. Renewable differ in many respects from fossil fuels, and these differences will have geopolitical consequences.

First, renewable energy resources are available in one form or another in most countries, unlike fossil fuels which are concentrated in specific geographic locations. This reduces the importance of current energy choke points, such as the narrow channels on widely used sea routes that are critical to the global supply of oil.

Second, most renewable take the form of flows, whilst fossil fuels are stocks. Energy stocks can be stored, which is useful; but they can be used only once. In contrast, energy flows do not exhaust themselves and are harder to disrupt.

Third, renewable energy sources can be deployed at almost any scale and lend themselves better to decentralized forms of energy production and consumption. This adds to the democratizing effects of renewable energy.

Fourth, renewable energy sources have nearly zero marginal costs, and some of them, like solar and wind, enjoy cost reductions of nearly 20% for every doubling of capacity.42 This enhances their ability to drive change but requires regulatory solutions to ensure stability and profitability in the power sector.

The energy transformation will be one of the major elements that reshape geopolitics in the 21st century, alongside trends in demography, inequality, urbanization, technology, environmental sustainability, military capability, and domestic politics in major states. •

World Solar Potential:

•Figure 1.0

•World Wind Potential
•Figure 1.1

REMEMBER TRADITIONAL GEOPOLITICAL IDEAS AND CONCEPTS :

Looking at geopolitics from a historic point of view, this area is also of strategic importance, as it is the centre of the Euro-Asian continent.

The great British geopolitical thinker Sir Harold Mackinder argued that the eastern maritime coalition should underline the importance of the Eurasian 'heartland' (including both, Central Asia and the Caspian Sea region) and predicted that Moscow's victory in World War II would make the USSR the greatest land power on the globe which could dominate Eurasia (and the world). After World War II, U.S. security planners (based on Mackinder's theories) saw the Soviet Union - as the 'heartland' power - as the fundamental threat to U.S. security interests; this led to the containment policy directed against Soviet geographic and ideological expansion during the so-called Cold War era. The Central Asia/Caspian Sea region belongs to Mackinder's 'heartland', but according to him, the basic element for global domination was the control over

eastern Europe. (Whoever controls eastern Europe rules the
'heartland', whoever rules the 'heartland', rules the 'world island'; and whoever rules the 'world island', rules the world.) Central Asia is an important, but not the essential, part of the heartland, according to Mackinder.

However, this was very certainly only true of Russia, or rather, the former Soviet Union, and possibly former Germany; according to Mackinder, the 'heartland' was impregnable to a seapower. These are hypotheses, and Spykman, for example, expanded on Mackinder's analysis by stating that whomever controls the (Eurasian) 'rimland' controls Eurasia, and whoever controls Eurasia, controls the world's fates. As a result, US foreign policy had to make it impossible for the Eurasian landmass to contain a disproportionately powerful power in Europe and the Far East. Especially, it should prevent a hostile, totalitarian nation from establishing political or military control over central Eurasia plus any substantial parts of the Eurasian 'rimlands'.

The Soviet involvement in Afghanistan, in which it backed the pro-Soviet state against various rebel forces, can be viewed as an attempt to seize control of a significant portion of the 'rimland.' Central Asia was, of course, the starting point for that endeavour. Control over Central Asia is still geopolitically important, however the need for continuous Western focus on the Eurasian 'heartland' has diminished as a result of several countries' (re)gaining independence from Russia, and the 'heartland' is no longer under the dominance of one hegemony. In the longer run, the geopolitical importance of this area could increase because the Eurasian 'rimland' still abounds in potential threats to world order.

CONCLUSION :

Geopolitics has mostly been about rivalries between great powers and their contestations of power on the large scale. These specifications of the political world focus on states and perpetuation of threats mapped as external dangers to specifically pacific polities. Much geopolitical disclosure specifies the world as a dangerous place, one supposedly necessitating violence in what passes for a realist interpretation of great powers as the prime movers of history.

It shows the spatial implications of sovereign nations, the vitality of their economies and their people's activities and influence over national borders and international relations. It shows us the struggle for power among nations.

References:

Importance of natural resources: https://www.fairobserver.com/region/north_america/geopolitics-natural-resources/

Why renewables will transform geopolitics: https://www.irena.org/-

/media/Files/IRENA/Agency/Publication/2019/Jan/Global_commission_geopolitics_new_wo rld_2019.pdf

Remember traditional geopolitical ideas and concepts:

https://www.bundesheer.at/pdf_pool/publikationen/09_sb1_05_egg.pdf

Micro-Entrepreneurship Preparing For the Future

Ms.Pihu Goel

Author Bio: Ms.Pihu Goel is a dedicated student currently pursuing grade eleven at G.D. Goenka Public School. She has opted the Commerce stream and aims to fulfil the aspirations that she has set for herself.

She has always had a passion for writing and is now on the path of pursuing writing in the journalism world as a full-time career. She started writing to jot down her emotions and opinions. Over time her writing skills improved and henceforth started writing for her school magazine's opinion column in grade eight. For the most part, she has written non-fiction and persuasive pieces about matters she strongly believe in as of now as that's her forte. Being appreciated for years for her writing skills by family and teachers, she planned to start a personal blog after grade ten which is now out there in the world.

Besides this, she has constantly been involved in extracurriculars. She holds a Limca book of record in Abacus, has won gold and silver in Asian Skating Competitions and several others. She is a member of the

World Cube Association. She believes that the credit for all that she has accomplished till day and is yet to achieve goes to her parents and the school where she spent every day learning and inculcating new skills.

Micro-Entrepreneurship: Preparing For the Future

ABSTRACT:

This study aims to provide a better understanding of why entrepreneurial education needs to be taught in educational institutions. A structure to introduce such a curriculum is also suggested. Further, the study goes about the question of why people need to be Micro - entrepreneurs rather than conventional employees. Articles, scholar papers, research papers were used to analyse, find out, and validate the same. Moreover, this study enhances one's knowledge of the new-age skills and their importance in the practical world today. It also goes over the statistics of employees and entrepreneurs in the world. The study educates one on how entrepreneurial education not only helps one in their career but also helps students graduate.

"innovation ready". (Friedman, 2013)

INTRODUCTION:

In the present circumstances, the structure of the workforce and its concepts have transformed due to the COVID-19 disruptions. Pandemic has disrupted the normal business activities and companies are made to invest in technologies to enable newfound ways of working. Companies have discovered modern and advanced arrangements in accomplishing their results. Consequently, this has brought in a new form of stability to the organizations. Organizations have realized that disruptions can be regular and need to be managed. The next few years are likely to be a harbinger of fast-paced changes. This massive change has brought an introduction of concepts like a blended workforce to achieve a competitive advantage. The gig force which was largely supplemental has embarked on to a mainstream role, involving high-skilled jobs. This newfound structure continues to grow post-pandemic and enforces individuals to adapt to the inevitable ways to ensure long-term viability. This shift has forced individuals to be micro-entrepreneurs. Nowadays workers/employees are made to focus on key areas like creating a web presence, negotiating ambiguity, effectively using mentors or influencers, and accessing an executional framework to sustain themselves. These activities centre on the challenges an employee has to overcome, and in the process, transition into to become a well-off micro-entrepreneur. Micro Entrepreneurs face difficulties in getting help as they are not formally recognized which can provide greater access to resources. With the increasing shift in the type of workforce, individuals need to be formally introduced to these concepts. As the situation is becoming the norm, educational institutes have a responsibility to prepare students for the brave new world. One wherein they're more likely to become Micro entrepreneurs rather than conventional employees. Business training needs to be a core curriculum in higher educational institutes to prepare students for the new brave world. In this article, we provide a structure to introduce such a curriculum and a model to help in institutionalizing the same.

LITERATURE REVIEW:

An entrepreneur is a person who earns a living by a start-up or by running businesses, all the while taking financial risks. The process of ushering in a business is known as entrepreneurship. Entrepreneurship Education provides students with knowledge, new-age skills, and inspiration to stimulate entrepreneurial success and intention in various ways. It acts as a muse and fosters intentions in people to establish a new business or idea. Entrepreneurship Education nurtures new-age skills in students. It counsels one on the skills of innovation, creativity, teamwork, network building, determination, and risk propensity. The skills one needs to become a ground-breaking empire builder are no longer generic. Instead, technical capabilities (social media management, big data analysis, programming, software knowledge, etc.) and human skills (training & development, organizational development, sales and marketing, vocational skills, human connections, etc.) will make progress (World Economic Forum, 2018).

The factor that people have knowledge of technology and business is essential, but the ability to inquire, cross-examine, comprehend the problem, and assertively communicate it, all the while being cooperative is more crucial. The ability to critically analyse the problems and solve them is a prerequisite. As Pete Drucker said, — "The only skill that will be important in the 21st century is the

skill of learning new skills. Everything else will become obsolete over time."
Entrepreneurship does not have much to do with money, but more to do with attitude, personality, and thinking. An entrepreneurial mind set is one when people believe in their ability to flourish, have goals, have a ground-breaking personality, are solutionoriented, reliable, and resourceful. Successful entrepreneurs are embarked as people with critical thinking, and people with individuality. Entrepreneurship Education influences people with these skills and drives entrepreneurial intentions in them as a result. Nelson (1977) attested that personality traits influence a person's decision to start a business. In view of the above research, the need for new-age skills in the practical world is clear. Presently, new-age skills are a prerequisite to survive in the practical world and get a promising career and life. Entrepreneurial education teaches students just that and also gives them a glimpse of the world.

The generation today is too engrossed in social media, and consequently has a bundle of expectations built up for how life should be but doesn't do anything to realize them. They don't have experience of the practical world. At the end of their schooling, most of the students don't have a clear-cut career choice or an idea of what they want to do.
The children today are living under an umbrella with almost no worries and goals. Consequently, they follow what their parents desire, and most of them end up being conventional employees. According to the stagnant curriculum that exists today in most schools, even the children with entrepreneurial skills end up being

conventional employees.

They don't want to take risks and hence don't become the doers, makers, and creative people that the world needs. This generation likes to take on challenges which is what the world needs today. But they don't have the guidance or resources to do it the right way. This is why entrepreneurial education is necessary for educational institutions today.

Being an entrepreneur is precarious but very remunerative and thrilling if executed the right way. There is no cap to an entrepreneur's potential. If a business is well established and thriving then for an entrepreneur, the sky's the limit. Whereas, for an employee, the earning potential is less as one gets just the salary and bonus. The promotions in a firm are not regular and often salary is not increased much. Even if one might be giving their best and earning a good amount, it becomes difficult for an ambitious employee to thrive in a regressive and stand pat atmosphere. On the other hand, an entrepreneur builds his links, connections, takes risks, progresses, bears the risks, and represents their own business. A total of 295,834 companies exported goods from the United States in 2015. Of these, 97.6% were in fact small businesses, for a total of 287,835 businesses. Despite the large number of entrepreneurs in the United States, these small businesses only made 32.9% of the country's total export income – $1.3 trillion (Dragomir Simovic, 2019). 35% of employees working at firms with 50 or fewer employees say they will likely pursue self-employment and 25% of people who work for larger companies are interested in pursuing entrepreneurship (FreshBooks, 2019). 78% of small business owners say their businesses are profitable (Guidant Financial, 2019). In 2020, 317 million small businesses in the United States accounted for 99.9% of businesses (SBA Office of Advocacy, 2020).

Entrepreneurship makes an immense contribution to the economy. Audia, Locke, and Smith (2000) pointed out that entrepreneurship is an important factor for the development of an economy.

The business operation is not a cakewalk. It's a dynamic, complex, competitive, and unpredictable territory. Many entrepreneurs start a business not because it's a calling, but, rather as a fall back option. But this doesn't make one a successful entrepreneur. An entrepreneur has to reckon with these forces, have a passion for business, and be adept in entrepreneurial behaviour. Entrepreneurs face a lot of challenges and need to have the will and ability to overcome these challenges to succeed. Entrepreneurial competencies can be defined as fundamental characteristics of pervasive and specific knowledge, aims, traits, self-images, interpersonal roles, and skills which result in setup birth, survival, and/or growth (Bird, 1995). An entrepreneur is an initiative, persistent, curious, passionate, perfectionist, committed, determined, systematic, assertive, confident, problem solver, they stop and smell the roses — these are some of the competencies of an entrepreneur.

Some of the public and private schools have fortunately

started realizing the value of entrepreneurial education. They have started having students do projects in groups to inculcate values of teamwork and problem-solving. But, it's not enough. A proper structure and model are required for the same. The great investment in entrepreneurship education in colleges and universities does not significantly improve the entrepreneurial rate of college students (Shen, Chen, & Chen, 2010). A specific model is needed to inculcate entrepreneurial behaviour in students.

METHODOLOGY:

Through the study, the question of why entrepreneurial education needs to be taught in educational institutions is dealt with. Further, the study goes about the question of why people need to be Micro - entrepreneurs rather than conventional employees. In addition, the study deals with the new-age skills and their importance in the practical world today. It also goes over the statistics of employees and entrepreneurs in the world. The study educates one on how entrepreneurial education not only helps one in their career but also helps in personality development.

The study is majorly based on a Qualitative approach. The qualitative approach has to do with the "what", "how" and "why" of opinions, mind sets, and beliefs. Qualitative data is generally in the form of writings, photographs, videos, and audios. Articles, scholar papers, research papers were used to analyse, find out, and validate the study.

This approach was adopted as it gives detailed descriptions of people's experiences, opinions, and perceptions which the Quantitative approach doesn't. At various points, the Quantitative approach is also adopted as statistics make the study more reliable which the qualitative approach alone doesn't. Quantitative research is the process of collecting, organizing, analysing, and interpreting numerical data. Various entrepreneurial statistics and surveys on the web were referred to and briefly analysed for the study.

CONCLUSION:

In conclusion, Micro-entrepreneurship is the future. One needs to teach the new generation and prepare them for the practical world. Entrepreneurial education needs to be inculcated in the school curriculums. Generation Z being conformists are not taught that taking risks is necessary today. So, they need to be guided the right way for a bright future ahead. It nurtures new-age skills in students. It counsels one on the skills of innovation, creativity, teamwork, network building, determination, and risk propensity. The curriculum that exists at the moment won't graduate the doers, makers, and creative people that the world needs. People need to become micro entrepreneurs today, not just conventional employees. Entrepreneurship is though a precarious career option, but a much more lucrative and rip-roaring one if brought about properly. Entrepreneurship is an important factor for the development of an economy. It's not just a cakewalk and requires entrepreneurial competencies. An entrepreneur should be an initiative, persistent, curious, passionate, perfectionist, committed, determined, systematic, assertive, confident, problem solver. They stop and smell the rose. They need to be highly competent. In order to prepare for the future of both oneself and the world, entrepreneurial education is a subject that should be built in the school just as much as one needs to be taught their native language.

SUGGESTIONS:

Rajeev Ranjan said, "Life skills are the art of living, which help us to draw personal and professional sketches of life". At present, there exist various enabling courses for almost all possible life skills. Life skill of problem solving makes a person inquisitive and proactive. Courses like Engineering Mathematics, Finite Automata and Formal Languages, Design and Analysis Of Algorithms, Discrete Mathematical Structures, Lean Startup Management. Creative and Social Enterprises: Business Models, Value and Planning, Essentials of Entrepreneurship: Thinking and Action, Mini Project • Ideation Lab, Innovation & Entrepreneurship - From Design Thinking to Funding could prove to be very helpful. Similarly, for the skill of teamwork, networking, coalition building courses like Principles of Entrepreneurship Management, Digital Marketing, Business Communication Lab are productive. Furthermore, there exist courses for life skills of critical thinking, people management, negotiation, service orientation, judgement and decision making, creativity, emotional intelligence, Cognitive Flexibility, etc.

References:

Bosma, N. and Kelley, D. (2018). Global Entrepreneurship Monitor Global Report. [online] .

Available at: https://www.gemconsortium.org/file/open?fileId=50213.

Dragomir Simovic (2019). 39 Entrepreneur Statistics You Need To Know In 2020. [online]

SmallBizGenius. Available at: https://www.smallbizgenius.net/by-the-numbers/entrepreneurstatistics/#gref.

FreshBooks (2019). 3rd Annual American Self-Employment Report | FreshBooks Research. [online] FreshBooks. Available at: https://www.freshbooks.com/press/annualreport [Accessed 4 Jul. 2021].

Friedman, T.L. (2013). Opinion | Need a Job? Invent It. The New York Times. [online] 30 Mar. Available at: https://www.nytimes.com/2013/03/31/opinion/sunday/friedman-need-a-jobinvent-it.html [Accessed 4 Jul. 2021].

Guidant Financial (2019). 2019 Small Business Trends & Statistics | Guidant Financial. [online] Guidant Financial. Available at: https://www.guidantfinancial.com/small-businesstrends/.

SBA Office of Advocacy (2020). 2020 Small Business Profile. [online] . Available at: https://cdn.advocacy.sba.gov/wp-content/uploads/2020/06/04144224/2020-Small-BusinessEconomic-Profile-US.pdf.

World Economic Forum (2018). The Future of Jobs Report 2018 Centre for the New Economy and Society. [online] . Available at: http://www3.weforum.org/docs/WEF_Future_of_Jobs_2018.pdf.

Appendix

INDEX

Glossary

Glossary attached in every chapter of the book.

Bibliography

Bibliography attached in every chapter in the book

List of Contributors

The book is written by Goenkans Edited by Dr. Priyanka Raheja, Co-edited by Ms. Manjari Arora , Student Editor is Ms. Vanshika Bansal & Illustrator is Ms.Ramya Arora. The books all authors(Mr.Jai Aneja,Ms.Priyanshi Gupta,Ms.Vanshika Bansal,Mr.Ayan Jain,Samarth Sarthak Shandilya,Ms. Saniya Gupta,Ms.Ishanvie Bansal,Ms.Mehak Malhotra,Ms.Tanisha Poddar,Mr.Raghav M Garg,Ms.Uditi Gupta,Ms.Mehak Gupta, Ms.Anya Jain , Ms.Pihu Goel) are from G.D.Goenka Public School Rohini, Sector 22, Delhi (India).

Notes

ISL Publications is a Global firm working on Publications, Research Development, Think-tank, Policy Research, Innovation Development, Publication, Legal, Media, Consulting, Coaching, Technology, Academic, Social Development, Communication, and Advisory & other areas of various Future Business, Educational, Technological, Social solutions.

www.ingramcontent.com/pod-product-compliance
Lightning Source LLC
LaVergne TN
LVHW100327181026
850499LV00039B/1009